THE ITALIAN

BAKER

MELISSA FORTI

THE ITALIAN BAKER

MELISSA FORTI

100 INTERNATIONAL

Baking Recipes

WITH *A*

MODERN TWIST

photography

DANNY BERNARDINI

quadrille

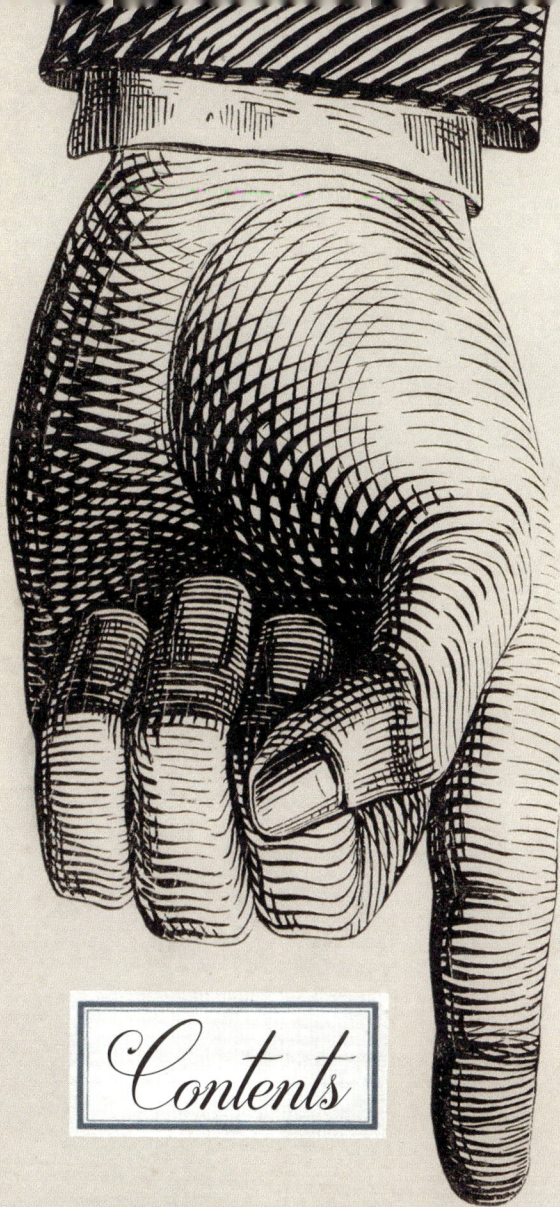

Contents

Introduction

I have been a professional baker for more than six years now. Since my first attempt, a lot has happened and many cakes have been baked! I moved to Sarzana, a small town in the region of Cinque Terre in the north west of Italy and started my first bakery. Since Day One my aim has been to offer real food to real people. I searched for recipes from the area and revisited recipes picked up on my travels around the world, adapting them for Italian tastes. I bake every morning to sell in the afternoon, everything is prepared from scratch and freshly baked, and the recipes change every day. This is so important to me – it is the core of my business and my way of living. Thankfully, organic produce is widely available here and I am so lucky to be able to have constant access to some of the best products available in the region and throughout Italy.

Recently, we moved to a bigger site in Sarzana and I am now the proud owner of a tea room, right in the historic and charming city centre, called Melissa's Tea Room & Cakes. It is a lifelong dream come true and I couldn't be happier to serve the wonderful customers who visit us every day in search of a moment of peace and delight.

I once found this quote left by a former flatmate in our flat in London: "If we don't get lost, we will never find a new route". I have travelled many roads, met many fascinating people and learnt from them. This book is who I am, it's what I love to do and, most of all, it is about how I see the world – a place where style, flavour, authenticity and attention are the most important ingredients. I hope you have as much fun making these recipes as I did writing them for you.

Yours truly, Melissa.

RECIPE NOTES:

I recommend organic, unwaxed citrus fruits when using the zest. ○ All eggs are large unless otherwise specified. ○ Recipes were tested in a fan-assisted (convection) oven. ○ Recipes give both metric and imperial/cup measurements. Please stick to one type of measurement when following a recipe and do not switch between metric and imperial/cups, as this will affect the results of your baking.

An

ASSORTMENT

of recipes

DALL'ITALIA

from *my country*

ITALY

CIAMBELLONE DEGLI ANGELI ITALIANO

ITALIAN ANGEL FOOD CAKE

I scour the internet for old baking books and vintage magazines for my collection, and I found this recipe in an Italian food magazine dated 1955. You can find real gems in old publications; some recipes need adjusting, some can be changed entirely and improved upon, but many are precious just as they are. They speak of a time that no longer exists, bringing you back to old traditions and telling you so much about the baking world of those bygone years.

This recipe is reliable and versatile, and needed no adjustments, so here it is as it appeared in the original magazine. Use it as a base for different fillings and decorations, drizzle over a fruit purée to soak in, or serve it simply as it is. Happy vintage baking to you all!

Serves 10–12

Ingredients

A little softened butter, for greasing

A little caster (*granulated*) sugar, for dusting

100g (*¾ cup plus 1 tablespoon*) plain (*all-purpose*) flour

95g (*¾ cup*) potato flour

2 teaspoons baking powder

10 egg whites (separated into 6 and 4 whites)

1 teaspoon vanilla paste or extract

350g (*scant 3 cups*) icing (*confectioner's*) sugar, plus extra for dusting

A pinch of salt

250g (*1 cup plus 2 tablespoons*) butter, melted

Method

Preheat the oven to 180°/350°F. Butter the insides of an angel food cake tin, about 24cm/9½ inches in diameter, (deep with a hole in the centre) and sprinkle caster sugar inside to coat.

Sift the flour, potato flour and baking powder three times into a bowl and set aside.

In the bowl of a stand mixer or in a mixing bowl and using an electric hand-held whisk, whisk 6 of the egg whites with the vanilla and icing sugar until stiff.

Put the remaining 4 egg whites into another bowl with the salt and, using thoroughly cleaned whisk attachments, whisk until stiff. Using a spatula, very gently fold this mixture into the egg white and icing sugar mixture until combined.

Now slowly start adding the sifted dry ingredients a little at a time, folding them very, very gently into the mixture. Finally, add the melted butter and fold into the mixture very gently. Pour the mixture into the prepared tin and bake for 30–40 minutes until golden and cooked through.

Once baked, leave to cool for 10 minutes in the cake tin before inverting on to a wire rack to cool completely. Dust with icing sugar, and/or fill or decorate if you like.

CUCCÌA AL VINO COTTO

This Sicilian dessert, served for the feast of Santa Lucia on 13 December, has no translation, and I have included it for two reasons. The first is that Sicily is a cross between tradition and internationality; it's well known that many Sicilians left Italy to move abroad and exported their cuisine all over the world. People from Sicily are proud people, proud of their heritage and yet open to the world at the same time.

The second reason is that the recipe was generously passed to me by a wonderful Sicilian who owns a restaurant, the Trattoria Marzocco, in a lovely Tuscan town called Pietrastanta, and it is one of my all-time favourite places to eat. It was his grandmother's recipe, and so should be cherished and respected. Thank you Pino!

Serves 10–12

Ingredients

450g *(1lb)* ricotta cheese, ideally sheep's milk, or cow's if sheep's isn't available

155ml *(⅔ cup)* double *(heavy)* cream

2 tablespoons icing *(confectioner's)* sugar

200g *(7oz)* mini chocolate chips (or chopped dark chocolate)

200g *(7oz)* cooked wheat (see Note)

250g *(1¼ cups)* caster *(superfine)* sugar

160ml *(⅔ cup)* red wine

1 teaspoon ground cinnamon

Method

Put the ricotta in a bowl and crush it using a fork, then press it into a second, large bowl through a very fine sieve so that it is lump-free and fluffy. Using an electric whisk, whisk the cream until thickened but not stiff. Give the ricotta a stir, then fold in the whipped cream and the icing sugar.

Stir in the chocolate chips, then the cooked wheat, and place in the fridge.

Put the sugar, wine and cinnamon into a pan set over a medium heat. Cook until the sugar has dissolved and the consistency resembles a syrup. Take off the heat and leave to cool, then chill in the fridge.

Serve the chilled ricotta mixture in cups or ramekins, or on small plates. Pour over the wine glaze to serve.

Note: Cooking wheat it is a time-consuming process, so I recommend you buy it precooked (available in many supermarkets). If you want to dive straight into the Sicilian tradition, follow these steps: Soak 70g (2½oz) wheat grain in a bowl of water for 5 days, changing the water a couple of times, then drain, rinse, put into a pan. Cover with about 700ml (3 cups) water and cook, covered, for 1 hour. Take off the heat and leave to stand, with the lid on, for 4 hours, then add the same amount of water as before and cook for a further 4 hours, adding more water if the pan starts to dry out. Once cooked, drain well. You should get about 200g (7oz) cooked wheat.

TORTA CAPRESE

FLOURLESS CHOCOLATE CAKE

The story goes that in 1920 in a bakery on the island of Capri, a pastry chef called Carmine Fiore created, by accident, a flourless cake that would become one of the most appreciated cakes of its time, *la torta caprese*. He had been commissioned to prepare a walnut cake for Al Capone, who came to Italy to buy gaiters in large quantities. Perhaps the chef was distracted or nervous, because he forgot to add flour to the cake, but the gangster loved the results so much he wanted the recipe to take home with him.

So here it is, in all its fame and glory! So simple and yet so rich. I've come across many different versions of this around the world, but this is the real deal.

Serves 8–10

Ingredients

230g *(1 cup)* butter, at room temperature, plus extra for greasing

200g *(7oz)* good-quality dark chocolate

200g *(1 cup)* caster *(superfine)* sugar

5 eggs, separated

35g *(⅓ cup)* good-quality cocoa powder

500g *(1lb 2oz)* chopped walnuts

2 teaspoons bicarbonate of soda *(baking soda)*

Icing *(confectioner's)* sugar, for dusting

Method

Preheat the oven to 180°C/350°F. Butter the insides of a 23-cm/9-inch springform cake tin and line with baking parchment.

Grate the chocolate or crumble it into little pieces in a food processor.

In the bowl of a stand mixer, or in a mixing bowl and using electric hand-held beaters, beat the butter and sugar together until pale and fluffy. Beat in the egg yolks, one at a time. Once well blended and creamy, beat or fold in the cocoa powder. Use a spatula to fold in the chopped walnuts and chocolate. Sift in the bicarbonate of soda and stir to combine.

Whisk the egg whites in a stand mixer or by hand until stiff. Fold into the cake mixture, trying not to knock any air out. Pour into the prepared tin and bake in the oven for 40–45 minutes until the edges have started to come away from the side of the tin. Once baked, leave to cool completely in the tin before transferring it to a serving plate.

Sprinkle with icing sugar and serve.

Note: I also sometimes add 1½ teaspoons espresso powder to the mixture (just before adding the egg yolks). Why? Because I'm Italian! Trust me, the result is sublime...

PASTIERA NAPOLETANA

Italian sun, tradition, Naples, the Costiera Amalfitana, Sorrento... they are all here in this recipe. A cross between a pie, tart and cake, the *pastiera* is quintessential Italy. Queen Maria Theresa of Habsburg, Holy Roman Empress in the 18th century, was known as "the Queen who never smiled", and the story goes that this pie was the only thing that would make her smile with delight.

Serves about 10

Ingredients

For the pastry

140g (*½ cup plus 2 tablespoons*) butter, chilled and diced, plus extra, softened, for greasing

235g (*1⅔ cups*) plain (*all-purpose*) flour, plus extra for dusting

130g (*1 cup*) icing (*confectioner's*) sugar

3 egg yolks, plus extra to glaze

1 teaspoon vanilla paste or extract

For the filling

240g (*8oz*) cooked wheat (see page 14)

100ml (*scant ½ cup*) milk

250g (*1¼ cups*) caster (*superfine*) sugar

A pinch of salt

3 tablespoons butter

450g (*1lb*) ricotta cheese

40g (*⅓ cup*) icing (*confectioner's*) sugar

Grated zest of 1 lemon

Grated zest of 1 orange

2 tablespoons orange blossom water

1 teaspoon vanilla paste or extract

1½ teaspoons ground cinnamon

3 eggs

120g (*4oz*) candied fruit, cut into small pieces

Method

Butter a 23-cm/9-inch springform cake tin and dust with flour.

For the pastry, pulse the flour and butter in a food processor until the mixture resembles fine breadcrumbs. Add the icing sugar, 3 egg yolks and vanilla and process just until the mixture comes together into a dough; do not over-process. Place the dough on the work surface and knead briefly, then wrap in cling film and refrigerate for up to 3 hours.

Roll out the chilled dough on a very lightly floured surface to a thickness of about 5mm/¼ inch. Leaving a circle large enough to line the tin, cut off 8 strips of pastry and set aside in the fridge. Lay the rest of the dough in the tin and press it neatly around the base and sides of the tin. Using a fork, prick the base in a few places, then chill the pastry case in the fridge while you make the filling.

Preheat the oven to 180°C/350°F. For the filling, heat the cooked wheat and milk in a saucepan set over a medium heat until it starts to boil, then add the caster sugar, salt and butter and stir until melted and creamy, about 15 minutes. Remove from the heat and set aside to cool. Press the ricotta through a fine sieve into a large bowl and add the icing sugar. Stir together until creamy, then add the lemon and orange zest, orange blossom water, cinnamon and eggs and stir to mix. Finally, add the cooled, cooked wheat mixture and the candied fruits and stir to combine. Pour the filling into the pastry case and place the strips of pastry in a lattice pattern over the filling, pressing the ends onto the pastry edges to seal. Brush the lattice strips with extra egg yolk to glaze. Bake in the oven for about 40–45 minutes until the pastry is golden and the filling set.

BACI DI ALASSIO

KISSES OF ALASSIO

Alassio is a charming town in Liguria where my uncle used to live, in a small apartment overlooking the sea. I also have a good friend from there, so thanks to both uncle and friend I have become addicted to these little treats! They are tiny moments of pure pleasure.

Perfect all year round, but amazing to nibble at a cocktail party or simply enjoyed on a rainy midweek evening in front of the TV, they are pure comfort food. Warning: high risk of overdose!

Makes about 20

Ingredients

240g (*8oz*) hazelnuts

35g (*⅓ cup*) good-quality cocoa powder

250g (*1¼ cups*) caster (*superfine*) sugar

3 egg whites

A pinch of salt

2 tablespoons clear honey

For the ganache

80ml (*⅓ cup*) double (*heavy*) cream

80g (*3oz*) good-quality dark chocolate, chopped

Method

Preheat the oven to 180°C/350°F. Line a baking sheet with baking parchment. Spread the hazelnuts out on the lined sheet and toast in the oven until they have released their oil, about 10 minutes. Remove from the oven and leave to cool completely. Transfer the cooled hazelnuts to a food processor, add the cocoa powder and sugar and pulse to a fine powder. Place a clean sheet of baking parchment on the baking tray; set both aside.

Put the egg whites and salt in the bowl of a stand mixer (or use a mixing bowl and electric hand-held whisk) and whisk until stiff. Very gradually fold in the hazelnut and cocoa mixture, then the honey. Pour the mixture into a piping bag fitted with a medium, fluted nozzle and pipe small rounds onto the lined baking sheet, leaving space between each to allow for spreading as they cook. Transfer to the oven and bake for 15 minutes, then remove the baking sheet to a wire rack and leave to cool.

Meanwhile, to make the ganache, bring the cream to a boil in a saucepan over a medium heat and, as soon as it reaches boiling point, take off the heat and add the chocolate. Leave to melt undisturbed for a few minutes, then stir to mix. Leave at room temperature until cool to the touch, then transfer to the bowl of a stand mixer (or use a mixing bowl and electric hand-held whisk) and whisk for 2 minutes on a high speed until smooth and thick.

Fill a clean piping bag with the ganache and pipe small dollops onto the bases of half the baked rounds. Sandwich together with the remaining rounds, as for a macaroon. Chill in the fridge and take them out just before serving.

TORTA MIMOSA
MIMOSA CAKE

I was born in the Eternal City of Rome. Every year for my birthday, my mother used to buy a mimosa cake from Euclide, one of the best pastry shops in the city. Their cake was a little different from the traditional recipe that involves pineapple chunks and orange blossom syrup – they made it with chopped strawberries and chocolate chips or shavings, which is how I still prefer it. Mimosa cake, so called as it is made to resemble the tropical mimosa flower, is famous in Italy for being the cake dedicated to women on International Women's Day on 8 March. I have fond memories of this cake and, even now, it is still my birthday cake of choice.

Serves 8

Ingredients

For the chantilly cream
240ml (*1 cup*) milk

Seeds of ½ vanilla pod

115g (*½ cup plus 1 tablespoon*) caster (*superfine*) sugar

2 egg yolks

Scant 3 tablespoons plain (*all-purpose*) flour, sifted

180ml (*¾ cup*) double (*heavy*) cream

For the sponge
4 whole eggs plus 8 egg yolks

200g (*1 cup*) caster (*granulated*) sugar

200g (*1½ cups plus 2 tablespoons*) plain (*all-purpose*) flour

30g (*¼ cup*) cornflour (*cornstarch*)

1 teaspoon vanilla paste or extract

For the syrup
180ml (*¾ cup*) water

180g (*¾ cup plus 2 tablespoons*) caster (*granulated*) sugar

1 tablespoon Kirsch liqueur (or 1½ tablespoons cherry juice for an alcohol-free syrup)

To assemble
About 340g (*12oz*) strawberries

Juice of ½ lemon

1 teaspoon caster (*granulated*) sugar

250g (*9oz*) chocolate chips

Method

First, prepare the chantilly cream. Pour the milk into a pan over a medium heat and add the vanilla seeds (scraped from the pod). Heat gently until it comes to a slow boil, then remove from the heat. Meanwhile, put the sugar and egg yolks in a bowl and, using an electric whisk, whisk until pale and light. Add the flour and whisk. Add some of the just-boiled milk to the yolk mixture, whisking on a low speed. Add the remaining warm milk and pour the mixture back into the pan. Cook over a gentle heat, whisking constantly with a balloon whisk until it thickens, about 3 minutes. Pour into a bowl, cover with cling film (plastic wrap) and cool completely before refrigerating for at least 30 minutes.

Whip the cream until stiff peaks form. Using a spatula, fold the whipped cream into the cold crème pâtissière until fully incorporated. Refrigerate. For the sponge cakes, preheat the oven to 180°C/ 350°F. Line two 23-cm/9-inch cake tins with baking parchment. Put the whole eggs and sugar into the bowl of stand mixer fitted with a whisk attachment, or in a mixing bowl and use a hand-held electric whisk, and start whisking on a low speed, increasing the speed to high for at least 10–15 minutes or until pale, creamy and quadrupled in volume. Add the egg yolks and continue whisking.

Double sift the flour with the cornflour and, using a spatula, fold gently into the egg mixture, taking care not to knock any air out. Divide the mixture between the prepared tins and bake for 30 minutes until a skewer inserted in the middle comes out clean. Cool slightly before inverting on to a wire rack to cool completely.

Meanwhile, to make the syrup, put the water, sugar and Kirsch into a pan over a medium heat. Let the sugar dissolve without stirring, then remove from the heat and leave to cool.

Finely chop the strawberries, add the lemon juice and sugar, stir and set aside. To assemble, take one of the cooled sponge cakes, trim any dark area from the top and sides using a serrated knife, then cut the circle of cake into 1.5-cm/⅔-inch cubes. Cut the other sponge in half horizontally, to give 2 thin sponges. Place one on a cake stand and brush the base generously with the syrup. Spread a layer of chilled chantilly cream over the sponge, top with the strawberries and chocolate chips and place the second thin sponge on top. Cover the entire cake with the remaining chantilly cream. If it is still soft, refrigerate the cake for 30 minutes. Finish by covering the entire surface with the sponge cubes, concentrating on the top to give it a slightly domed shape.

CASTAGNACCIO

This is the simplest cake in the world to make, and one of the oldest, dating back in Tuscany to the 1500s. When I was a little girl my mother used to make it during the first days of autumn. At the time I didn't appreciate the simplicity of the cake, a child's tastebuds being more attuned to fruity and chocolatey things, but growing up I have learned to love *castagnaccio*. With its nutty, earthy flavours, I would call it a "cake for grown-ups". It is perfect served with some whipped ricotta and honey, or paired with a glass of Vin Santo.

Makes 2 small or 1 large cake

Ingredients

2 tablespoons olive oil, for greasing

500g *(1lb 2oz)* chestnut flour

A pinch of salt

750ml *(3 cups plus 1 tablespoon)* water, at room temperature

75g *(3oz)* walnuts, chopped

50g *(2oz)* pine nuts

65g *(2½oz)* raisins

Method

Preheat the oven to 200°C/400°F. *Castagnaccio* is a very shallow cake, and you can use either two 23-cm/9-inch shallow cake tins or 1 pizza pan. You can make it rectangular if you like too, but if you want to go with tradition, go for shallow round. Generously oil the chosen tin/s, tapping away any excess oil, and set aside.

Sift the chestnut flour into a large bowl, add the salt and slowly add the water, whisking constantly using a balloon whisk. The batter should be completely lump-free, smooth and creamy.

Pour the batter into the prepared tin/s and sprinkle the walnuts, pine nuts and raisins evenly over the top. Bake for 20–25 minutes or until you see cracks all over the surface. Serve at room temperature.

SALAME DI CIOCCOLATO

CHOCOLATE SALAMI

A classic for the festive holidays, but also a great and fun treat for any time of the year. Take it with you on a picnic in the country, or eat it sliced at the end of a meal, with a glass of dessert wine. It is pure comfort food. Not for those on a diet, but I always say that it's better to have a little healthy homemade treat than lots of store-bought candies! It is an Italian recipe that has become an international one. Feel free to personalize it by adding new ingredients every time! Did I mention that there is no baking involved, and it is also an egg-free recipe?

Makes 15–20 slices

Ingredients

100g (*1/3 cup plus 1 1/2 tablespoons*) butter

250g (*9oz*) dark chocolate, chopped

250g (*9oz*) digestive biscuits or Graham crackers, roughly crushed

85g (*3oz*) blanched almonds, roughly chopped

2 tablespoons honey

2 tablespoons good-quality cocoa powder

2 tablespoons rum

Icing (*confectioner's*) sugar, to finish

Method

Put the butter and chocolate in a heatproof bowl and microwave until melted.

In another bowl, combine the crushed digestive biscuits, almonds, honey, cocoa powder and rum. Stir in the melted chocolate and butter mixture, until completely incorporated.

Lay a large piece of baking parchment on the work surface and spoon the mixture on top. Now start working the dough with your hands, shaping it into a log. Once in a rough log shape, wrap the log up in the baking parchment and roll it, using your hands, to set and neaten the shape. Twist the ends of the parchment in opposite directions, as for a candy or sweet.

Put the salami the fridge for at least 4 hours to set. Once hardened, unwrap it and dust all over with icing sugar. Cut into slices to serve.

SCHIACCIATA CON NOCCIOLE E MORE

CRUSHED DOUGH WITH HAZELNUTS AND BLACKBERRIES

This is a recipe inspired by a traditional "cake" from Tuscany, *schiacciata all'uva*. I say "cake", because this preparation is closer to a sweet focaccia than a cake, and it also reminds me of pizza, due to the type of dough used. In Tuscany they make *schiacciata all'uva* using the same quality of grapes used to make Chianti wine. As grapes are not easy to find when not in season, let alone Chianti grapes, I came up with this variation to give you all the possibility of trying it at home. But if you happen to own a vineyard or you live in Tuscany and can get hold of the right quality of grapes, then be my guest and substitute grapes for the blackberries used here.

Serves 6–8

Ingredients

10g (*1/3oz*) fresh yeast, cut into small pieces

180ml (*3/4 cup*) lukewarm water

300g (*scant 2 1/2 cups*) plain (*all-purpose*) flour

1 teaspoon salt

3 tablespoons caster (*granulated*) sugar, plus extra for sprinkling

3 tablespoons extra virgin olive oil

220g (*8oz*) ground hazelnuts

400g (*10 1/2oz*) fresh blackberries

Method

Put the yeast in a small bowl, add the water and stir until the yeast has completely dissolved. Place the flour, salt and sugar on the work surface and, using your hands, mix together into a mound. Make a well in the centre and pour the yeast mixture into the well, along with the oil.

Using your hands, or a bread scraper, work the ingredients together to form a dough, then knead in the ground hazelnuts. Add a little extra flour if the mixture is too sticky. Form the dough into a ball, place in a large bowl and cover with a cloth. Put the bowl in a warm place and leave to prove until doubled in volume, about 1 hour.

Preheat the oven to 180°C/350°F. Line a lipped baking tray, 20 x 30cm/8 x 12 inches, with baking parchment and press the dough directly onto the tray, spreading it over the entire surface of the tray using your hands, but without kneading it; just press it inside the tray. Drop the blackberries onto the dough like a rain shower, sprinkle some sugar all over and bake in the oven for about 15 minutes, until lightly golden and springy to the touch.

Leave to cool before cutting into squares to serve.

PARROZZO

Parrozzo is a dome-shaped dessert that dates back to the time when a famous Italian poet called Gabriele D'annunzio wrote about the cake created to celebrate the shape and colour of the bread made by farmers using cornflour. You can find it in the Italian region of Abruzzo, especially at Christmas, or better still you can make your own. It is divine poetry!

Serves 6–8

Ingredients

80g (⅓ cup) butter, melted, plus extra, softened, for greasing

Good-quality cocoa powder, for dusting

100g (3½oz) blanched almonds

60g (½ cup) cornflour (cornstarch)

60g (½ cup) plain (all-purpose) flour

5 eggs, separated

1 teaspoon vanilla paste or extract

130g (½ cup plus 2 tablespoons) caster (granulated) sugar

200g (7oz) good-quality dark chocolate, cut into small pieces

Method

Preheat the oven to 180°C/350°F. Butter the inside of a dome-shaped mould and dust with cocoa powder.

Finely chop the almonds (or pulse in a food processor until coarsely chopped). Sift both flours and set aside.

In the bowl of a stand mixer (or using a mixing bowl and an electric hand-held whisk) whisk the egg yolks, vanilla and sugar until pale and tripled in volume.

Add the melted butter, the chopped almonds and sifted flours and fold in gently.

Whisk the egg whites until stiff, using an electric mixer or whisk, and fold them into the mixture. Pour into the prepared mould and bake for 40 minutes until a skewer inserted in the middle comes out clean. Leave to cool in the mould for 15 minutes before inverting on to a wire rack, dome side up, and leaving to cool completely.

Melt the chocolate, leave to cool slightly, then pour it all over the cooled cake. Allow to set at room temperature.

BISCOTTI CANESTRELLI

CANESTRELLI COOKIES

I'm again going to have to start with "When I was a little girl"… I'm sorry, but I do believe that for us bakers and food lovers the best memories always come from deep in the past. So, here goes: when I was a little girl, many desserts, cookies or candies were forbidden, so every time I was allowed to have something sweet my taste buds would go crazy! I remember the local bakery in Rome near my house baking these cookies. There were small and would fit perfectly into a little girl's hand… Because they are baked in a shape of a flower with a hole in the middle, the game was to eat 10 cookies, one from each finger, and consequently become completely covered in sugar. Ah, my mum was so happy about that!

Canestrelli ("little baskets") come from the Piedmont and Liguria regions and are similar to *ovis mollis* (see page 48) but the different ratios give a different texture and flavour. The recipe apparently dates back to the Middle Ages, and has been much appreciated ever since.

Makes about 40

Ingredients

6 hard-boiled egg yolks

330g *(2⅓ cups)* plain *(all-purpose)* flour

180g *(1½ cups)* potato flour

120g *(1 cup)* icing *(confectioner's)* sugar, plus extra for dusting

300g *(1⅓ cups)* butter, at room temperature

1 teaspoon vanilla paste or extract

Method

Using a fork, press the egg yolks through a fine mesh sieve directly into the bowl of a stand mixer fitted with a paddle attachment. Alternatively, you can use a mixing bowl and a wooden spoon.

Sift both flours and the icing sugar into the bowl and slowly beat them into the egg yolks. Add the butter and vanilla and beat until the mixture forms a dough. Wrap in cling film (plastic wrap) and chill in the fridge for 1 hour.

Meanwhile, preheat the oven to 160°C/320°F and line a baking sheet with baking parchment. Roll the chilled dough out to a thickness of about 1cm/⅓ inch. Using a 4- or 5-cm/1½- or 2-inch flower shaped cutter, stamp out about 40 cookies. Transfer to the lined baking sheet and make a hole in the centre of each cookie using a medium piping nozzle.

Bake for about 15 minutes until cooked but still very pale. Remove and leave to cool on the baking sheet. When completely cool, dust the tops generously with icing sugar.

Note: For a lovely gift, place the cookies in a metal tin and wrap with a pretty ribbon. They will last a little more than a week.

MERINGHE BRUTTE MA BUONE ALLE NOCCIOLE

UGLY-BUT-GOOD HAZELNUT MERINGUES

The best hazelnuts come from the Piedmont region of Italy. They are pure gourmet pleasure and can be used in hundreds of different ways. Always look for *"nocciole di Piemonte"* – many delicatessens around the world sell them. These meringues, as their name suggests, are not attractive, but they are indeed delicious. They keep for months stored in a jar, so you can bake them way in advance.

Makes about 20

Ingredients

240g *(8oz)* blanched hazelnuts, ideally from Piedmont

4 egg whites

¼ teaspoon cream of tartar

200g *(1 cup)* caster *(granulated)* sugar

1 teaspoon vanilla paste

Method

Preheat the oven to 135°C/275°F. Line a large baking sheet with baking parchment.

Put the hazelnuts into a food processor and pulse until coarsely chopped; you are looking for a mixture of powder and chunks.

Put the egg whites and cream of tartar into the bowl of a stand mixer, or into a mixing bowl and use an electric hand-held whisk, and whisk until frothy. Add the sugar in small additions, whisking constantly until stiff peaks form.

Gently fold the ground hazelnuts and vanilla paste into the meringue using a spatula, taking care not to deflate the mixture. Using a spoon, drop dollops of meringue onto the lined baking sheet, leaving space between each meringue to allow room to expand as they bake.

Bake for 30 minutes until soft on the inside and crisp on the outside. Leave to cool before serving.

CIAMBELLINE AL VINO ROSSO

RED WINE DOUGHNUT COOKIES

While living in Rome at the age of six, I used to run down to the local grocery shop and buy these delicious crunchy cookies, made by the owner's wife following the traditional Italian recipe from the Lazio region. In the old days, they would be eaten at Christmas, but they are so good they can now be found all year round. Happy me!

Makes about 20 large cookies

Ingredients

175ml (¾ *cup*) olive oil

400ml (1⅔ *cups*) full-bodied red wine

650g (5½ *cups*) plain (*all-purpose*) flour, plus extra for dusting

170g (¾ *cup*) granulated sugar, plus extra for dusting

½ teaspoon bicarbonate of soda (*baking soda*)

2 teaspoons ground aniseed

1 teaspoon vanilla extract

A pinch of salt

Method

Pour the oil and wine into a jug or bowl and stir to combine. Put the flour in a mound on the work surface and make a well in the middle. Add the sugar, bicarbonate of soda, star anise, vanilla and salt to the well and carefully pour in the oil and wine mixture.

Using your hands, slowly combine all the ingredients to create a dough. If the dough is too sticky, add a little more flour, but not too much or the result will be a dry and tough dough. Place the dough in a bowl, cover with a tea towel and leave to rest for 30 minutes. Meanwhile, preheat the oven to 180°C/350°F and line a large baking sheet with a sheet of baking parchment.

Taking one small piece of dough at a time, roll it into a sausage about 8cm/3 inches long (or 10cm/4 inches if you would prefer bigger cookies), then join the ends by pinching them together. Dust with sugar and place on the lined baking sheet. Repeat with the remaining dough, making sure they are not too close to each other on the sheet or they will stick (use 2 baking trays if necessary).

Bake for about 15 minutes until cooked and nicely golden on top.

Note: In Italy we dunk these in a glass of wine at the end of a meal. Kids can enjoy them with a glass of milk, perhaps, and although there is wine in the dough, you won't get them drunk as the alcohol cooks off in the oven. So, no worries!

BISCOTTI ALL'OLIO EXTRA VERGINE D'OLIVA

EXTRA VIRGIN OLIVE OIL COOKIES

Cookies like this will put a smile on the face of every dairy-intolerant person. The recipe originally comes from Tuscany where fragrant olive oil is widely produced. It is such a big deal around there that we tend to use it more than we do butter. These cookies are great dunked in cold milk or simply eaten as they are. They also have a good shelf life, stored in a jar or tin.

Makes about 30

Ingredients

170g (1¼ *cups*) plain (*all-purpose*) flour, plus extra for dusting

100g (¾ *cup*) potato flour

100g (½ *cup*) caster (*granulated*) sugar

A pinch of salt

2 egg yolks

Finely grated zest of 2 lemons

1 teaspoon vanilla paste or extract

1½ tablespoons water

100ml (⅓ *cup plus* 1½ *tablespoons*) extra virgin olive oil

Method

Put the flour, potato flour, sugar and salt in a large bowl, and stir to combine. Make a well in the centre and add the egg yolks, lemon zest, vanilla and water. Beat gently, using a fork. Add the olive oil and bring all the ingredients together into a dough. Using your hands, knead the dough until smooth and elastic, then wrap in cling film (plastic wrap) and refrigerate for at least 30 minutes.

Meanwhile, preheat the oven to 170°C/335°F and line a large baking sheet with baking parchment.

Roll the rested dough out on a lightly floured surface to about a 4-mm/⅛-inch thickness. Stamp out cookies using a small or medium cutter of your choice and bake for 10–15 minutes or until lightly golden. Leave to cool on the baking sheet.

BISCOTTI CANTUCCINI

For us Italians there is always a good excuse to have food and wine together, and it is a solid tradition to match the right food with the right wine – a serious matter. These *biscotti* come from Tuscany and are well known all over the world, usually eaten at the end of a meal between dessert and coffee, and traditionally while sipping a velvety dessert wine called Vin Santo. In fact, in Chianti no meal ends without *cantuccini e Vin Santo*! Stored in an airtight tin or jar, they will last for over a month.

Makes about 20

Ingredients

300g *(scant 2½ cups)* plain *(all-purpose)* flour

½ teaspoon bicarbonate of soda *(baking soda)*

A pinch of salt

200g *(1 cup)* caster *(granulated)* sugar

Finely grated zest of 1 orange

1 teaspoon aniseeds

4 eggs, lightly beaten

150g *(5oz)* almonds

Method

Preheat the oven to 190°C/375°F. Line a large baking sheet with baking parchment.

Mix the flour and bicarbonate of soda together and place in a large bowl. Add the salt, sugar, orange zest, aniseeds and three quarters of the beaten eggs. Knead together to form a dough. If it seems too hard to work with, add a drop of room temperature milk.

Knead the almonds into the dough to incorporate. Shape into a ball and cut into 3 pieces, then shape each piece into a log, each the same length. Place the logs on the baking sheet, leaving some space between them. Brush each log with the remaining beaten egg and bake for 15 minutes. Remove from the oven and, using a serrated knife, cut the logs at an angle (they will be piping hot, so be careful) into slices about 1cm/⅜ inch thick. You should get about 10 biscotti from each log. Place each cut slice flat on the same baking sheet, return to the oven and bake for a further 5 minutes.

Remove from the oven and leave to cool.

CROCCANTE ALLE MANDORLE

ALMOND BRITTLE

This doesn't involve baking as such, but is so yummy I had to include it in the book. I would call it a treat, or a sin actually, due to the amount of sugar in it. Its origins are not very clear. Some say it was invented by the Spanish during the second half of the 15th century. Others credit it to the Italians, but one thing is sure, the famous Italian writer and gastronomist Pellegrino Artusi decided to include the recipe in his great book *"La scienza in cucina e l'arte di mangiar bene"* (*Science in the kitchen and the art of eating well*), published in 1800.

I had the best *croccante* while in one of my favourite restaurants, Ottone Primo, in Sarzana. They make an amazing thin and crispy *croccante* and it is to them that I dedicate my version. With a glass of fine dessert wine this makes the perfect ending to a good meal, and your friends will agree. Stored in an airtight container, it will keep for a long time.

Makes about 6 large pieces

Ingredients

Olive oil, for greasing

200g (*1 cup*) caster (*granulated*) sugar

1 tablespoon water

100g (*3½ oz*) blanched almonds

Method

Pour a little oil onto a large sheet of baking parchment and rub it over the entire surface. Set aside.

Place the sugar and water in a large skillet or frying pan set over a medium heat, making sure the sugar is spread in an even layer. Let the sugar melt, swirling the pan every so often but without stirring. It will take about 3 minutes for the sugar to turn golden.

Meanwhile, warm the almonds in a microwave or low oven to allow them to barely warm up but not toast (warming them avoids a cold ingredient coming into contact with the hot caramel). Once the caramel starts to turn golden, add the warmed almonds and stir to fully coat the almonds in the caramel. You don't want the caramel too brown or it will taste bitter.

Transfer the mixture to the oiled sheet of baking parchment and spread the caramel with a greased spatula until 1–1.5cm/⅜–⅔ inch thick. Take care, as it is still very, very hot at this stage. Leave to cool completely before cutting into shapes using a long knife or breaking into pieces. Arrange on a serving dish and enjoy.

TORTA DELLA NONNA
GRANDMA'S CAKE

In every culture, in every tradition, there is always a "grandma's cake". For some reason, things made by grandmothers always taste better. It's like an insurance for success: "If this is grandma's recipe, then you can be sure it's good". It's because things were once made with love, using real ingredients. Without being expert pastry chefs, our beloved grandmothers were able to impress the family on every occasion. And grandma's cooking stays with us for ever, becoming part of our heritage. We Italians are very proud of our grannies!

This cake, or rather tart, comes from Tuscany and was actually created by an Italian chef rather than a grandmother. But my grandmother used to make it, so to me it qualifies. It has many variations, such as the addition of cocoa powder (in which case it is called grandpa's cake) and is so famous where I live that you can find it in almost every restaurant.

Serves 8–10

Ingredients

For the pastry
300g (*scant 2½ cups*) plain (*all-purpose*) flour, plus extra for dusting

150g (*⅔ cup*) butter, chilled and diced, plus a little extra, softened, for greasing

120g (*½ cup plus 2 tablespoons*) caster (*granulated*) sugar

1 whole egg plus 2 egg yolks

A pinch of salt

Grated zest of 1 lemon

For the crème pâtissière
1 litre (*4 cups*) whole milk

Grated zest of 1 lemon

8 egg yolks

150g (*¾ cup*) caster (*granulated*) sugar

150g (*1¼ cups*) plain (*all-purpose*) flour

To decorate
120g (*4oz*) pine nuts

Icing (*confectioner's*) sugar

Method

Put the flour on the work surface. Add the chilled butter and, using your fingertips, rub into the flour until it resembles fine breadcrumbs. Mound up the mixture and make a well in the middle. Add the sugar, whole egg and extra yolks to the well, with the salt and lemon zest. Knead lightly to form a dough, then wrap in cling film (plastic wrap) and refrigerate for 1 hour.

Butter a 20-cm/8-inch round fluted tart tin with a removable base and dust with flour. Divide the dough in two, place one half in the fridge and roll the other half out to a thickness of about 3mm/⅛ inch. Use to line the tart tin, pressing the pastry gently into the grooves.

Make the crème pâtissière. Put the milk and lemon zest in a saucepan over a medium heat. Bring to a boil, then strain through a fine sieve into a bowl. Allow to cool.

Using a stand mixer fitted or an electric hand-held whisk, whisk the egg yolks and sugar until creamy and frothy. Gradually whisk in the flour. Pour the cooled milk back into the pan over a medium heat and add the egg and sugar mixture. Using a balloon whisk, stir constantly until the cream thickens. Pour the crème into a shallow bowl and cover with cling film, touching the surface to prevent a skin from forming. Refrigerate for 30 minutes. Preheat the oven to 170°C/335°F.

Remove the pastry case from the fridge and pour the crème pâtissière inside the case. Roll out the other half of dough to a circle large enough to fit over the tart. Place it over the tart, pressing the edges all around to seal (do this properly or the crème will seep out during baking). Sprinkle the pine nuts all over the surface and bake for 40 minutes, until the pastry is golden. Leave to cool, then dust with icing sugar before serving.

ZABAIONE

This is not a cake or cookies or other baking treat, but a versatile cream that is a cross between a pudding and a filling. It can be served in glasses or ramekins with lady fingers (see page 72) or fresh fruit, or used as a filling for cakes. The first published recipe in Italy dates back to 1662 and, because it is rich in protein, it was once served to invalids to restore strength and energy. As this recipe includes alcohol, I would consider it an adult treat. It is absolutely delicious and so easy to make!

Serves 4 as dessert, or enough to fill a 20-cm/8-inch cake

Ingredients

8 egg yolks

200g *(1 cup)* caster *(granulated)* sugar

8 tablespoons Marsala (or Port)

Cocoa powder, for dusting

Method

Put the egg yolks and sugar in a heatproof bowl set over a pan of simmering water, making sure the base of the bowl is not touching the water. Using an electric hand-held whisk, whisk to a smooth, pale cream.

Add the Marsala in a steady stream, whisking constantly. Cook, whisking, for 5–10 minutes until smooth and pale, then remove from the heat. Pour into individual glasses or ramekins and chill in the fridge for at least 1 hour before serving.

Sprinkle with cocoa powder and serve with lady fingers, fruits, chopped chocolate or just as it is.

OVIS MOLLIS COOKIES

These are probably among the best cookies in the world... or at least they are to me. They come from the north of Italy and the name literally means "soft egg" – their tender texture is achieved by using hard-boiled egg yolks as well as potato flour. Plain vanilla cookies, they are a hit in my tea room and can also be prepared as thumb-print cookies with jam. I like them plain, as I believe beauty and flavour hide in simple things.

Makes 25–30

Ingredients

100g (¾ cup) cornflour (cornstarch)

200g (1½ cups plus 2 tablespoons) plain (all-purpose) flour, plus extra for dusting

200g (scant 1 cup) butter, chilled and diced

100g (½ cup) caster (granulated) sugar

5 hard-boiled egg yolks

1 teaspoon almond oil or extract

1½ teaspoons vanilla paste or extract

Icing (confectioner's) sugar, for dusting

Method

Put both flours into a food processor and pulse to mix. Add the diced butter and pulse again until mixture resembles fine crumbs. Add the sugar and pulse again. Finally, add the egg yolks, almond oil and vanilla and pulse until the mixture forms a dough; don't worry if the mixture looks dry at first, keep the machine running for a little longer. Transfer the dough to the work surface and form it into a ball. Wrap in cling film (plastic wrap) and leave to rest in a cool place (not in the fridge) for about 1 hour.

Preheat the oven to 160°C/320°F and line a large baking sheet with baking parchment.

Sprinkle a little flour on the work surface and roll out the dough to about a 5-mm/¼-inch thickness. Traditionally, a ring cookie cutter with a hole in the middle is used, but choose a medium cutter you like and stamp out cookies from the dough. Place on the lined baking sheet, spacing them slightly apart, and bake for about 10 minutes or until lightly golden (take care not to over-bake).

Remove from the oven and allow to cool on the baking sheet. When completely cool, dust with a generous amount of icing sugar.

TORTA DELLE MONTAGNE

CAKE FROM THE MOUNTAINS

I have a kind of obsession for recipes from the Alps, and mountains in general. My father comes from the Friuli region in the north of Italy, so I guess a part of me belongs there, and my childhood fairytales were full of such recipes. For years I believed in gnomes who lived inside trees. My father would tell me stories of far-away lands in central Europe, of the Black Forest, and he gave me a book with illustrations showing mother-gnome baking for her children and family. She would go out riding a hare in search for the juiciest berries for her cakes, and would then bake the prettiest cake I had ever seen. I dreamed of doing the same one day.... Oh well, I guess in part I do, minus the hare ride!

This simple cake is so yummy, and will make you feel as though you were in a fairytale. The recipe comes from Trentino Alto Adige, a luscious region in the north of Italy. Use only the best ingredients, to capture the scent of the mountains, and top with fresh berries if you like.

Serves 8–12

Ingredients

250g *(1 cup plus 2 tablespoons)* butter, at room temperature, plus extra for greasing

Plain *(all-purpose)* flour, for dusting

250g *(2 cups)* buckwheat flour

100g *(3½ oz)* ground hazelnuts

1½ teaspoons baking powder

50g *(2oz)* breadcrumbs

1 teaspoon ground cinnamon

6 eggs, separated

1 teaspoon vanilla paste or extract

250g *(1¼ cups)* brown sugar

100ml *(scant ½ cup)* organic apple juice

250g *(9oz)* organic raspberry, blueberry or redcurrant jam

Icing *(confectioner's)* sugar, for dusting

Method

Preheat the oven to 170°C/335°C. Butter a 23-cm/9-inch springform cake tin and dust with a little flour.

Put the flour, ground hazelnuts, baking powder, breadcrumbs and cinnamon in a bowl and stir to combine.

In the bowl of a stand mixer, or in a mixing bowl and using electric hand-held beaters, beat the butter, egg yolks, vanilla and sugar together for about 20 minutes or until very creamy and increased in volume.

Beat the flour mixture and apple juice alternately into the egg yolk mixture in three additions, starting and ending with flour. In a separate bowl, whisk the egg whites to stiff peaks and gently fold them into the mixture. Pour into the prepared tin and bake for about 1 hour, until a skewer inserted in the middle comes out clean, and the edge of the cake is starting to come away from the side of the tin.

Leave to cool before removing the cake from the tin and cutting it in half horizontally. Spread the jam over one half and top with the other, then dust with icing sugar.

TORTA DI CAROTE ITALIANA
ITALIAN CARROT CAKE

I love a good, healthy carrot cake! At the bakery we make two versions of this: American-style with cream cheese frosting, and Italian-style. So let me introduce you to a wonderful breakfast or, even better, the ultimate afternoon comfort food while drinking a cup of tea.

Serves 8–10

Ingredients

75g (*⅓ cup*) butter, at room temperature, plus extra for greasing

100g (*¾ cup plus 1 tablespoon*) plain (*all-purpose*) flour, plus extra for dusting

1¼ teaspoons baking powder

Finely grated zest and juice of 1 orange

75g (*⅓ cup*) caster (*granulated*) sugar

2 eggs, separated

150g (*5oz*) peeled organic carrots, finely grated

65g (*2oz*) chopped almonds

5 teaspoons milk

Icing (*confectioner's*) sugar, for dusting

Method

Preheat the oven to 170°C/335°F. Butter the insides of a 23-cm/9-inch springform cake tin and dust with flour.

Sift the flour into a bowl and add the baking powder. Set aside.

Put the butter, orange zest and juice and half the sugar into a separate bowl and, using a balloon whisk, beat together. Add the egg yolks one at a time, then add the grated carrots and chopped almonds. Finally, add the flour and baking powder mixture in three additions, alternating with the milk. Do not over-mix.

In the bowl of a stand mixer, whisk the egg whites on a medium speed until foamy (or use a mixing bowl and an electric hand-held whisk). Add the remaining sugar and whisk to stiff peaks. Fold the egg whites into the cake mixture, transfer to the prepared tin and bake for 25–30 minutes until a skewer inserted in the middle comes out clean. Leave to cool in the tin before inverting on to a plate. Dust with icing sugar before serving.

LINGUE DI GATTO

CAT'S TONGUE COOKIES

These light, very thin, delicious little treats are adored by children and grown-ups alike, especially served with a big gelato or an espresso respectively. Super-easy to make and super-good!

Makes about 30

Ingredients

100g (⅓ *cup plus 1½ tablespoons*) butter, at room temperature

100g (¾ *cup plus 1 tablespoon*) icing (*confectioner's*) sugar

1 teaspoon vanilla paste or extract

1 teaspoon almond oil or pure extract

3 egg whites

100g (¾ *cup plus 1 tablespoon*) plain (*all-purpose*) flour

Method

Preheat the oven to 190°C/375°F. Line a baking sheet with baking parchment.

In the bowl of a stand mixer, place the butter, icing sugar, vanilla and almond oil. Beat until pale and fluffy. Start adding the egg whites a little at a time and, when incorporated, mix in the flour. Do not over-mix. (You can do all of this by hand if you prefer, using a wooden spoon and a mixing bowl.)

Transfer the mixture to a piping bag fitted with a plain medium nozzle and pipe shapes about 4cm/1½ inches long, leaving generous space between each. Bake for about 6–8 minutes or until turning golden on the edges. Leave to cool on the baking sheet.

TORTA DI SEMOLINO E RICOTTA

SEMOLINA AND RICOTTA CAKE

In Italy there are many recipes calling for ricotta or other cheeses, and the range of fresh organic versions available is amazing. Italians love their fresh cheeses, and I would say I was fairly addicted! Ricotta has a heavenly effect when mixed into desserts, and semolina creates a lovely texture. This will disappear very quickly, I assure you…

Serves 8

Ingredients

2 tablespoons butter,
  plus extra for greasing

250g (9oz) semolina flour,
  plus extra for dusting

1 litre (4 cups) cold milk

2 lemons, zest pared into strips
  from one, zest finely grated
  from the other

Pared zest of 1 orange

400g (14oz) ricotta cheese

6 eggs

1 teaspoon vanilla paste
  or extract

200g (1 cup) caster (granulated)
  sugar

A pinch of salt

Method

Preheat the oven to 180°C/350°F. Butter a 23-cm/9-inch springform cake tin and dust with semolina flour.

Put the milk into a saucepan and pour in the semolina flour. Stir to mix with a balloon whisk. Set the pan over a medium heat and add the pared lemon and orange zest. Cook, stirring constantly with the balloon whisk to avoid scorching, until starting to thicken, then remove and discard all the pared zest. Remove the pan from the heat and add the butter, stirring until melted. Set aside to cool.

Meanwhile, set a fine-mesh sieve over a large bowl and press the ricotta through using a spoon, to remove any lumps. Stir in the eggs and vanilla, then add the sugar, salt and the grated lemon zest. Now add the semolina and milk mixture and gently stir. Transfer the mixture to the bowl of a stand mixer fitted with a whisk attachment (or use a hand-held electric whisk) and whisk on a medium speed for about 3 minutes.

Pour into the prepared tin and bake for about 45 minutes or until dark golden on top. Leave to cool in the tin for 20 minutes before unmoulding to serve.

BISCOTTO DI SAVOIA

Despite the misleading name, this is not a biscuit (cookie) but a light and delicious cake.

This recipe goes back more than 85 years but is still modern and versatile. It has a dreamy texture, thanks to whisked egg whites and potato flour, and looks stunning as a festive centrepiece on any table. Decorate it with a crown of flowers or fresh fruit and you are all set! Play with the flavours according to the occasion or season: at Christmas, add cinnamon, raisins and other spices. For a summer party, add lemon zest or rose water.

Serves 10–12

Ingredients

A little softened butter, for greasing

100g (*about ¾ cup*) potato flour, sifted, plus extra for dusting

180g (*6oz*) egg whites (about 5 large)

¼ teaspoon cream of tartar

240g (*2 cups*) icing (*confectioner's*) sugar, sifted, plus extra for dusting

120g (*4oz*) egg yolks (about 6)

1 teaspoon vanilla paste or extract

1 teaspoon almond oil or pure extract

70g (*scant ½ cup*) plain (*all-purpose*) flour, sifted

Method

Preheat the oven to 170°C/335°F and lightly butter a Bundt or pandoro tin. Dust a little potato flour into the tin and set aside.

Place the egg whites and cream of tartar in the bowl of a stand mixer fitted with the whisk attachment (or use a mixing bowl and electric hand-held whisk) and whisk until foamy. Slowly add 40g (⅓ cup) of the sifted icing sugar and continue to whisk until stiff peaks form. Set aside.

Place the egg yolks, vanilla and almond oil in the cleaned bowl of the stand mixer, or a separate bowl and use an electric hand-held whisk. Beat until pale. Add the remaining sifted icing sugar and gently beat until fully incorporated. Fold the whisked egg whites into the yolk mixture, until completely blended.

Finally, fold in both sifted flours very gently. Pour the batter into the prepared tin and bake for about 40–45 minutes. Leave to cool in the tin for at least 15 minutes before unmoulding. Once completely cool, decorate the top as you wish, with a dusting of icing sugar over the cake.

A
SELECTION

of recipes

DAL MONDO

from *around* the

WORLD

FOCACCIA ALLA PORTOGHESE

PORTUGUESE STYLE SWEET FOCACCIA

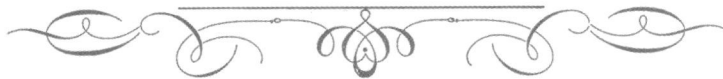

For years this was the snack I took to school. My mother used to buy it at our local bakery and would put a couple of tiny sponge squares into my lunchbox. It was a real treat. Ever since then, whenever I bake them the aroma they produce takes me back in time, to those sweet days… The name is a bit of a mystery, but could be to do with Portuguese merchants who brought the recipe with them when they arrived in Italy around the end of the 1400s.

You can make this in a round tin, but for sentimental reasons I stick to the square shape of my childhood. It is usually simply dusted with icing sugar, but here I drizzle an orange syrup over the cake and top with fruit.

Makes 4 squares

Ingredients

For the sugar syrup
200ml *(¾ cup plus 1 tablespoon)* water

200g *(1 cup)* caster *(granulated)* sugar

1 tablespoon orange juice

For the cake
A little softened butter, for greasing

150g *(1 cup)* ground almonds

50g *(⅓ cup)* potato flour

150g *(¾ cup)* caster *(granulated)* sugar

Finely grated zest and juice of 2 oranges

3 eggs, separated

¼ teaspoon cream of tartar

Method

For the syrup, put the water and sugar in a pan over a medium heat and bring gently to a boil until the sugar has completely dissolved. Remove from the heat, immediately add the orange juice and set aside to cool. (Leftover syrup can be stored in the fridge for a couple of weeks.)

Preheat the oven to 150°C/300°F. Butter the insides of a 20-cm/8-inch square tin and line with baking parchment.

Put the ground almonds and potato flour into a food processor and pulse until very fine. Sift the mixture and process again, then tip into a bowl and set aside. Without washing the food processor, add the sugar and orange zest and process until well blended and fine.

In the bowl of a stand mixer fitted with a whisk attachment (or use a mixing bowl and hand-held electric whisk), whisk the egg whites and cream of tartar until stiff and glossy, then set aside. In a separate bowl, whisk the egg yolks until pale and doubled in volume. Stir in the sugar and orange mixture.

Using a spatula, fold the almond and potato flour mixture into the yolk mixture and combine well. Add the orange juice and stir. Finally, very gently fold in the egg whites, making sure you don't deflate the batter.

Pour into the prepared tin and bake for about 35–40 minutes until a skewer inserted in the middle comes out clean. Leave to cool in the tin for 15 minutes before inverting on to a wire rack. While still warm, brush the top with the orange syrup. Leave to cool before cutting into squares. Serve with fruit scattered on top.

TORTA AL CIOCCOLATO E LAMPONI

CHOCOLATE AND RASPBERRY CAKE

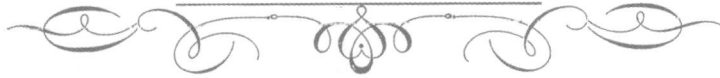

This is a classic at my bakery, with customers ordering it for weddings, birthdays and dinner parties. While I was living in Los Angeles, I couldn't resist a twice-weekly trip to a local café to eat the best chocolate cake I have ever tasted, served in gigantic slices… Back home, I have tried and tried to replicate it, and this is the closest I can get to the original. I'm very proud of the results. I use raspberry coulis, but you can substitute other fruits and the result will be still be amazing!

Serves 12

Ingredients

245g (1¾ cups) plain (all-purpose) flour, plus extra for dusting

3 eggs

240ml (1 cup) buttermilk

240ml (1 cup) warm water

120ml (½ cup) vegetable oil

1 teaspoon vanilla paste or extract

400g (2 cups) caster (granulated) sugar

80g (¾ cup) good-quality cocoa powder

2 teaspoons baking powder

1 teaspoon bicarbonate of soda (baking soda)

A pinch of salt

For the raspberry coulis

100g (½ cup) caster (granulated) sugar

3 tablespoons water

340g (12oz) frozen raspberries, thawed

1 teaspoon raspberry *eau de vie* (or other raspberry liqueur)

For the chocolate frosting

170g (6oz) softened butter, plus extra for greasing

105g (1 cup) good-quality cocoa powder

80ml (⅓ cup) milk

560g (4⅔ cups) icing (confectioner's) sugar, sifted

Method

Preheat the oven to 180°C/350°F. Lightly butter the bases and sides of two 20-cm/8-inch cake tins and dust with flour.

Place the eggs, buttermilk, warm water, oil and vanilla in a large bowl. Sift together the sugar, flour, cocoa powder, baking powder, bicarbonate of soda and salt and add to the liquid mixture.

Divide batter between the prepared tins and bake for 35 minutes until a skewer inserted in the middle comes out clean. Leave to cool in the tins for 10 minutes before inverting on to a wire rack.

For the coulis, heat the sugar and water together in a small saucepan over a medium heat, until the sugar has completely dissolved, about 10 minutes. Let the syrup cool a little then pour it into a blender and add the raspberries. Pulse to a purée then strain through a sieve to remove the seeds. Stir in the eau de vie and chill in the fridge for at least 30 minutes.

Make the chocolate frosting. In the bowl of a stand mixer fitted with a paddle attachment, beat the softened butter. Add the cocoa powder and beat for 10 seconds. Add a little of the milk, then a little of the icing sugar and continue adding these alternately, beating until creamy. If the mixture is too runny, add more icing sugar; if it is too stiff add more milk. You are looking for a good, spreadable consistency.

To assemble the cake, place one cake on a plate. Brush the entire surface with the raspberry coulis, letting it penetrate into the cake to make it soft and full of flavour. Spread on some of the chocolate frosting and stack the other cake on top. Using an off-set spatula, spread the rest of the frosting over the top and sides of the cakes.

TORTA DI MORE ALLA SCOZZESE

SCOTTISH BRAMBLE CAKE

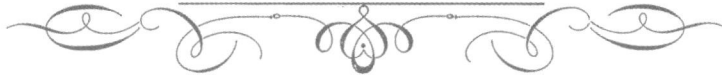

I simply LOVE Scotland! On a summer trip I visited the charming town of Pitlochry in the Southern Highlands, where I had the chance to try this delicious cake. No matter where I go I have to visit the local bakery and try new things, but there is an unspoken law among bakers that you never ask for a recipe unless it is given to you as a gift. I wasn't offered this recipe and so I came up with my own version. Here it is: a tribute to one of the most wonderful places I have ever seen, and a place I will surely visit again. Aye!

Serves 6–8

Ingredients

230g (*1 cup*) butter,
  plus extra for greasing

About 250g (*9oz*) blackberries

80ml (*⅓ cup*) Vin Santo or
  other sweet dessert wine

115g (*½ cup plus 1 tablespoon*)
  caster (*granulated*) sugar

2 eggs

450g (*3½ cups*) plain
  (*all-purpose*) flour

1 teaspoon baking powder

½ teaspoon bicarbonate of
  soda (*baking soda*)

80ml (*⅓ cup*) buttermilk

Icing (*confectioner's*) sugar,
  for dusting

Fresh berries, to decorate
  (optional)

Method

Preheat the oven to 180°C/350°F. Butter the insides of a deep, 18-cm/7-inch springform cake tin.

Wash the blackberries and pat them dry using kitchen paper, taking care not to damage or break them. Put into a bowl, stir in the Vin Santo, cover and leave to infuse for 15 minutes.

Meanwhile, in the bowl of a stand mixer (or using a mixing bowl and electric hand-held beaters) beat the butter and sugar together until pale and creamy. Beat in the eggs, one at a time.

Sift the flour, baking powder and bicarbonate of soda into a separate bowl and combine. Beat the dry ingredients into the creamed butter and sugar and, once incorporated, turn the mixer down to a low speed and pour in the buttermilk. Finally, using a spatula, gently fold in the blackberries and Vin Santo, trying not to break them too much.

Spoon the mixture into the prepared tin and bake for 30–35 minutes until golden and cooked, and a skewer inserted in the middle comes out clean. Invert on to a wire rack to cool, then dust with icing sugar and decorate with fresh berries, if you like. Serve with a luscious dollop of clotted cream, or mascarpone if you are in Italy...

LAMINGTONS

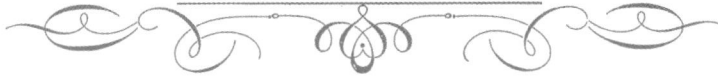

I discovered lamingtons on a trip I took to Australia, while driving from Adelaide to Melbourne. We stopped in what looked like a ghost town in the middle of the wildest outback, and I remember there wasn't much around, except a bakery. And so I went in and a lovely young girl suggested I buy one of her treats. I was amazed at how good it was! The girl asked what my job was and so I told her I was a baker too, and owned a bakery in Italy. She said: "Well, you like our lamingtons so much I will give you our recipe. Make them in Italy and spread the word"!

Australians fill their lamingtons with thick cream, but because it is impossible to find in Italy I fill mine with whipped cream, and the result is just as good.

Makes 18

Ingredients

A little softened butter, for greasing

140g (1¼ cups) plain (all-purpose) flour, plus extra for dusting

50g (⅓ cup) cornflour (cornstarch)

2 teaspoons baking powder

6 eggs, at room temperature

150g (¾ cup) caster (granulated) sugar

300ml (1¼ cups) double (heavy) cream

For the chocolate icing glaze

640g (4 cups) icing (confectioner's) sugar, sifted

55g (½ cup) good-quality cocoa powder

15g (½oz) butter, melted

250ml (1 cup) milk

225g (8oz) finely shredded desiccated coconut

Method

Preheat the oven to 180°C/350°F. Butter two 9-cavity mini loaf tins and dust with flour. Sift the flour, cornflour and and baking powder together three times and set aside.

In the bowl of a stand mixer, or in a mixing bowl and using a hand-held electric whisk, whisk the eggs on a high speed until silky, pale and tripled in size. Gradually whisk in the sugar until it is completely incorporated. Fold in the sifted flours and divide the mixture between the loaf cavities.

Bake for about 20 minutes until a skewer inserted in the middle comes out clean and the cakes are started to pull away from the sides of the tins. Remove from the oven and leave to cool for 10 minutes in the tins before inverting the lamingtons on to a wire rack to cool completely.

Meanwhile, for the icing, put the sifted icing sugar and cocoa powder in a heatproof bowl and set the bowl over a pan of barely simmering water, making sure the bowl is not touching the water. Stir in the butter and milk using a wooden spoon. Keep stirring until the mixture coats the back of the spoon.

Put the shredded coconut into a shallow bowl. Dip each cooled lamington in the icing then roll in the coconut to coat. Leave to set, then cut each one in half horizontally. You will now have 36 iced and coated sections. Place them cut side up on a large sheet of baking parchment. Whisk the cream until medium stiff. Fill a piping bag fitted with a large star-shaped nozzle with the cream and pipe it onto half of the sliced lamingtons. Put the remaining lamington halves on top to sandwich together.

CHARLOTTE AL CIOCCOLATO

CHOCOLATE CHARLOTTE

This is a variation on a French classic, but few people know that it was quite possibly the English who first made it, in honour of Queen Charlotte, wife of King George III, so it's another case of a perfect international blend of culture and tradition that I love.

You can use shop-bought lady fingers, but making them from scratch is much more rewarding, and since this recipe produces more than you actually need, you get to enjoy them any time of the day. They also go well with *zabaione* (see page 46), and they are happy to be frozen.

Serves 6–8

Ingredients

For the lady fingers

6 eggs, separated

¼ teaspoon cream of tartar

180g (¾ *cup plus 2 tablespoons*) caster *(granulated)* sugar

180g (1¼ *cups*) plain *(all-purpose)* flour, sifted

Icing *(confectioner's)* sugar, for dusting

For the chocolate filling

500g (1lb 2oz) good-quality dark chocolate, chopped into small pieces

1 litre *(4 cups)* double *(heavy)* cream

Good-quality cocoa powder, for dusting

Method

Preheat the oven to 160°C/320°F. Line two baking sheets with baking parchment.

Put the egg whites and cream of tartar in the large bowl of a stand mixer (or use a large mixing bowl and an electric hand-held whisk) and whisk until frothy, then add half the sugar in small additions, whisking until stiff peaks form. In a separate bowl, whisk the egg yolks with the remaining sugar until pale. Gently fold the whisked egg whites into the egg yolk mixture, then gradually fold in the flour to make a smooth, airy mixture.

Fill a piping bag fitted with 2-cm/1½-inch plain nozzle with the mixture. Pipe fingers 9cm/3½ inches long, leaving space between each as they will expand during baking. Dust with icing sugar and bake for 10 minutes, until lightly golden around the edges. Leave to cool on the sheets.

To assemble, sprinkle a little icing sugar onto the base of a 20-cm/8-inch springform cake tin. Stand the lady fingers vertically around the edge, so each one is just touching the next. Refrigerate.

Place the chocolate and a quarter of the cream in a heatproof bowl set over a pan of barely simmering water, making sure the bowl is not touching the water. Allow the chocolate to melt, stirring occasionally. Put the remaining cream in the bowl of a stand mixer fitted with the whisk attachment (or in a mixing bowl and use a hand-held electric whisk) and whisk it till barely thickened

Add the chocolate ganache to the thickened cream and stir to combine. Pour the mixture into the tin, inside the lady finger border, and put back in the fridge to set.

Once set, remove the sides of the tin. Tie a ribbon around the base if you wish. Dust with cocoa powder and add any decorations you like, such as berries, whipped cream or edible flowers.

TORTA DI ZUCCA SPEZIATA

SPICED PUMPKIN CAKE

This is not pumpkin pie as you know it. It is a lovely, dense and rich rustic cake, wonderful for a Sunday morning breakfast in autumn. It is delicately spiced and not too sweet, with the pine nuts contributing a slight crunch.

Serves 6–8

Ingredients

For the pumpkin

About 500g (*1lb 2oz*) pumpkin

100g (*½ cup*) caster (*granulated*) sugar

For the cake

100g (*⅓ cup plus 1½ tablespoons*) butter, at room temperature

200g (*1 cup*) caster (*granulated*) sugar

2 eggs

225g (*1¾ cups*) plain (*all-purpose*) flour, sifted

2½ teaspoons bicarbonate of soda (*baking soda*)

125ml (*½ cup*) milk, at room temperature

Finely grated zest of 1 lemon

1 teaspoon vanilla paste or extract

40g (*2oz*) pine nuts

Method

Preheat the oven to 180°C/350°F. Line a 20-cm/8-inch springform cake tin with baking parchment.

Deseed and peel the pumpkin, cut into chunks and spread out on a baking sheet lined with baking parchment. Sprinkle over the sugar and bake for 1 hour, until soft and cooked. Remove from the oven and allow to cool slightly. You want 150g (5½oz) cooked pumpkin for the recipe. Transfer the right amount to a sieve and press with the back of a spoon to extract some of the excess water. Transfer the pumpkin to a food processor and blend to a purée. Set aside.

In the bowl of a stand mixer fitted with the paddle attachment (or using a mixing bowl and a wooden spoon), beat the butter and sugar together until pale and creamy. Add the eggs, one at a time, and beat until the mixture is doubled in size. Fold in the sifted flour and bicarbonate of soda, then add the pumpkin purée and stir to combine. Stir in the milk, lemon zest and vanilla. Finally, fold in half the pine nuts.

Transfer the mixture to the prepared tin, sprinkle the remaining pine nuts all over the surface of the cake and bake on a lower shelf of the oven for about 40–45 minutes until dark golden and cooked through.

Leave to cool in the tin for 30 minutes before inverting on to a plate to serve.

MADELEINES ALLE ROSE

ROSE MADELEINES

I could eat madeleines all day, in every possible way. They are one of the first sweet treats I ever baked, and are easy and fun to make. Kids love making them as they are always a success.

You can glaze them with coloured royal icing or dip them in a light chocolate ganache, or simply dust them with icing sugar. You can also omit the rose water and keep them plain, or add some grated lemon zest. Whichever way, they are delicious.

Makes 24 small madeleines

Ingredients

125g *(generous ½ cup)* butter, melted, plus extra, softened, for greasing

105g *(¾ cup)* plain *(all-purpose)* flour, sifted, plus extra for dusting

85g *(⅓ cup plus 1 tablespoon)* caster *(granulated)* sugar

3 eggs

2 teaspoons rose *eau de vie*, pure rose extract, or rose water

1 teaspoon vanilla paste or extract

75g *(½ cup)* ground almonds

½ teaspoon baking powder

Method

Preheat the oven to 180°C/350°F. Butter and flour two 12-hole (small) madeleine tins.

Sift the measured flour twice and set aside. In the bowl of an electric mixer, or using a mixing bowl and electric hand-held whisk, whisk the sugar, eggs, rose and vanilla until light and creamy.

Add the sifted flour, ground almonds and baking powder and stir to combine. Finally, stir in the melted butter. Using a spoon, drop the mixture into the moulds, filling them almost but not quite to the top. Bake for 10 minutes until pale golden and cooked through.

LOAF AI LAMPONI

RASPBERRY STREUSEL LOAF CAKE

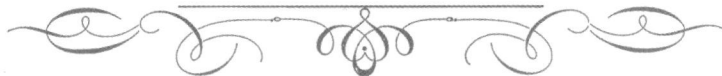

This recipe can be used as a base for many variations, with blueberries, blackberries or even apples in place of the raspberries. When I lived in Los Angeles, I used to often go to a café near Hollywood Boulevard to have a slice of this for breakfast with a cup of coffee. Few things work magically like raspberries, and they really are one of my favourite little fruits. If you bake this for a Sunday morning breakfast or picnic in the park, your family and friends will thank you!

Serves 8–10

Ingredients

For the streusel

75g (*½ cup*) plain (*all-purpose*) flour

6 tablespoons caster (*granulated*) sugar

115g (*½ cup*) butter, chilled and diced

For the cake

170g (*¾ cup*) butter, at room temperature, plus extra for greasing

340g (*2¼ cups*) plain (*all-purpose*) flour, plus extra for dusting

2½ teaspoons baking powder

250g (*1¼ cups*) caster (*granulated*) sugar

Finely grated zest of 1 lemon

1 teaspoon vanilla extract

3 eggs

175g (*¾ cup*) sour cream

250g (*9oz*) raspberries

Method

Preheat the oven to 180°C/350°F. Butter the base and sides of a 1lb loaf tin and dust with flour.

To make the streusel, put the flour, sugar and diced butter in a bowl and rub in the butter with your fingertips until the mixture resembles fine breadcrumbs. (You can do this in a food processor if you like.)

For the cake, sift the flour and baking powder into a bowl and set aside. Put the sugar and lemon zest into the bowl of a stand mixer (or into a mixing bowl and use electric hand-held beaters) and beat on a low speed. Add the butter and vanilla and continue beating until light and fluffy, then beat in the eggs one at a time, followed by the sour cream. When thoroughly combined, fold in the flour and baking powder mixture in three additions.

Using a spatula, fold in half the raspberries, taking care not to break them up. Pour the mixture into the loaf tin and top with the remaining raspberries, pressing them into the mixture a little. Sprinkle the streusel mixture evenly over the top and bake for about 40–45 minutes, until a skewer inserted in the middle comes out clean (except for some raspberry smears).

Leave to cool in the tin for 15 minutes before inverting on to a wire rack. Leave to cool completely before serving.

BROWNIES AL FORMAGGIO

CHEESECAKE BROWNIES

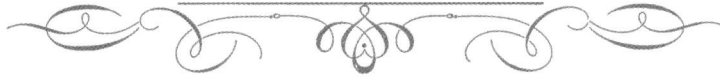

Many of my customers at the bakery and tea room absolutely love these brownies – maybe because they combine two of the most appreciated ingredients in baking: chocolate and cream cheese. Usually brownies call for dark chocolate and cocoa powder, but I leave out the chocolate as I like my brownies to stay soft when cold. Here the cream cheese adds a surprising texture, and the result is a double layer of delight!

Makes about 24, depending on size

Ingredients

For the cream cheese topping

120g (*½ cup*) butter, softened, plus extra for greasing

225g (*1 cup*) cream cheese, at room temperature

180g (*about ¾ cup*) caster (*granulated*) sugar

3 eggs

4 tablespoons plain (*all-purpose*) flour

2 teaspoons vanilla paste or extract

For the brownies

350g (*1½ cups*) butter, softened

500g (*2½ cups*) caster (*granulated*) sugar

150g (*1½ cups*) good-quality cocoa powder

6 eggs

200g (*1½ cups plus 2 tablespoons*) plain (*all-purpose*) flour

Method

Preheat the oven to 180°C/350°F. Butter a 30-cm/12-inch square baking tin and line with baking parchment.

For the topping, beat the butter and cream cheese together until creamy in the bowl of a stand mixer or using a mixing bowl and electric hand-held beaters. Add the sugar and eggs and beat until incorporated, then finally add the flour and vanilla and beat on a low speed until smooth. Set aside while you make the brownie mixture.

In a separate bowl, cream the butter and sugar together using an electric mixer. Add the cocoa powder and beat until fluffy. Add the eggs, one at a time, and finally add the flour. Spread three quarters of the mixture into the tin, using a spatula. Top with the cream cheese mixture and finish with the remaining brownie mixture. Run a cocktail stick (toothpick) or the tip of a sharp knife over the surface, to create a marbled effect.

Bake for 30–35 minutes until the brownies start to pull away from the sides of the tin, then leave to cool in the tin until still slightly warm before cutting into squares to serve. Or, for a more fudgy result, leave to cool completely and refrigerate before serving.

BLONDIES AI LAMPONI

RASPBERRY BLONDIES

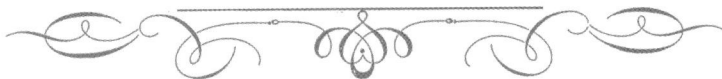

When it's not a chocolate fix you need, but something fresher and lighter, do not hesitate to bake these blondies! This version is something totally different from the original, with a cakey texture and with no white chocolate – as it isn't a true chocolate I avoid using it. Quick to make and even quicker to finish off…

Makes 12 large or 24 small squares

Ingredients

400g (1⅓ cups) butter, at room temperature, plus extra for greasing

450g (3½ cups) plain (all-purpose) flour, plus extra for dusting

200g (1 cup) caster (granulated) sugar

150g (scant ½ cup) light brown sugar

Finely grated zest of 3 lemons

1 teaspoon vanilla paste or extract

6 eggs

A pinch of salt

1 teaspoon baking powder

250g (9oz) raspberries

Icing (confectioner's) sugar, for dusting (optional)

Method

Preheat the oven to 180°C/350°F. Butter the insides of a 30-cm/12-inch square tin and dust with flour.

In the bowl of a stand mixer, or using a mixing bowl and hand-held electric beaters, cream the butter, both sugars, lemon zest and vanilla together until pale and fluffy. Beat in the eggs, one at a time.

Sift the flour into a bowl and add salt and baking powder. With the mixer or beaters on a low speed, gradually add the flour mixture until incorporated; do not over-beat. Spread the mixture into the prepared tin using a spatula. Press the raspberries into the mixture and bake for 30 minutes, until golden and cooked through.

Leave to cool in the tin before inverting on to a board and cutting into squares, adding a dusting of icing sugar if you like.

TORTA AI MIRTILLI E PANNA ACIDA

BLUEBERRY SOUR CREAM COFFEE CAKE

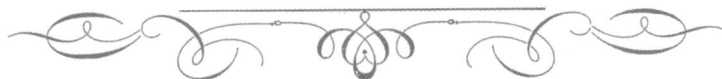

Blueberries love sour cream, and sour cream loves blueberries, and the result is an American classic. I once had a slice of this cake in New York, in a small café on Rivington Street, run by two girls. I don't remember the name of the café but I sure remember their cakes! Sorry girls, but if you ever read this book, thank you for inspiring me!

Serves 8

Ingredients

For the cake
200g *(scant 1 cup)* butter, at room temperature, plus extra for greasing

250g *(2 cups)* plain *(all-purpose)* flour, plus extra for dusting

200g *(1 cup)* caster *(granulated)* sugar

3 eggs

Finely grated zest of 1 lemon

1½ teaspoons vanilla paste or extract

2 teaspoons baking powder

155g *(⅔ cup)* sour cream, at room temperature

For the blueberry topping
4 tablespoons white sugar

4 tablespoons water

About 340g *(12oz)* fresh blueberries

Method

Preheat the oven to 160°C/320°F. Lightly butter the insides of a 23-cm/9-inch springform cake tin and sprinkle in some flour, tilting and rotating the pan until coated, then tipping out any excess flour. Sift the measured flour with the baking powder and set aside.

In the bowl of a stand mixer (or using a mixing bowl and electric hand-held beaters), cream the butter and sugar together until pale and fluffy. Beat in the eggs one at a time, then add the lemon zest and vanilla and beat on a medium speed for 3 minutes. Fold in one third of the sifted flour, followed by half the sour cream, then fold in another third of flour, followed by the remaining sour cream. Finally, fold in the remaining third of flour.

Transfer the mixture to the prepared tin and bake on the middle shelf for about 45 minutes until a skewer inserted in the middle comes out clean. Leave to cool in the tin for about 40 minutes before unmoulding. Place on a serving plate to cool completely.

Meanwhile, for the topping, put the sugar and water into a saucepan placed over a medium heat and allow the sugar to dissolve. Reduce the heat to medium-low and add the blueberries. Stir gently to avoid breaking up the berries, and cook until the juices are released and then thicken, about 5 minutes. The blueberries should be soft and not broken. Leave to cool completely.

Spoon the cooled blueberry mixture over the cake and serve.

Tip: Try sprinkling chopped walnuts over the blueberry topping, for a crunchy texture.

BUNDT CAKE AL WHISKEY E CIOCCOLATO
CHOCOLATE WHISKY BUNDT CAKE

My partner in life is a Scotch whisky lover and chocolate fanatic, and I cherish those winter nights in front of the fireplace drinking whisky together while he smokes a cigar. It's the best way to end a long day at work for me.

For this recipe I have used a classic after dinner malt whisky matured in fresh sherry casks, but you can choose whatever you like. The alcohol evaporates in the cooking process, but leaves behind its incredible aromas.

This cake is for you M, with all my love.

Serves 8–10

Ingredients

230g (*1 cup*) butter,
 at room temperature,
 plus extra for greasing

105g (*1 cup*) good-quality
 cocoa powder, plus extra
 for dusting

120ml (*½ cup*) Scotch whisky

400g (*2 cups*) caster
 (*granulated*) sugar

280g (*2 cups*) plain
 (*all-purpose*) flour

1¼ teaspoons bicarbonate
 of soda (*baking soda*)

1 teaspoon salt

2 eggs

1 teaspoon vanilla paste
 or extract

Icing (*confectioner's*) sugar,
 for dusting

Method

Preheat the oven to 160°C/320°F. Butter a bundt tin generously, making sure you coat the entire insides of the tin, then dust with cocoa powder.

Pour the whisky into a pan set over a medium heat, add the butter and cocoa powder and whisk, using a balloon whisk, until the butter is melted. Remove from the heat, add the sugar and stir until dissolved. Transfer to a large bowl so that it cools down more quickly.

Sift the flour, bicarbonate of soda and salt into a separate bowl and set aside.

Put the eggs and vanilla into the bowl of stand mixer, or a mixing bowl and use electric hand-held beaters, and beat for about 3 minutes. Add the cooled whisky and chocolate mixture and beat on a low speed until combined. Add the flour mixture and beat until incorporated. Pour the mixture into the prepared tin and bake for 40–50 minutes until a skewer inserted in the bundt comes out clean.

Leave the cake to cool completely in the tin before inverting on to a plate. Lightly dust with icing sugar, and serve with a dollop of whipped cream.

FINANCIERS

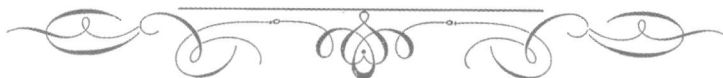

However much I enjoy making fancy cakes and bakes, I am just as fond of simple treats. The satisfaction that comes with successful baking is of course priceless but, more than that, I love the romantic, nostalgic feel of homemade cakes. They bring back memories, celebrate tradition and are part of our culture, passed through families from generation to generation.

I found this recipe for financiers, little French cakes, in an old baking book a friend bought for me, and I have adapted and simplified it to make it simpler and more homely. If you would like to follow the more traditional recipe, using *beurre noisette*, then see the Note opposite. You can also make them a bit more posh by serving them with warm custard and raspberries, adding blackberries to the middle of the batter, or dunking them in silky chocolate ganache once cooked. But, if you are like me, you will appreciate them with a simple dusting of icing sugar and a good cup of tea.

Makes 8

Ingredients

75g *(⅓ cup)* butter, plus 2 tablespoons for greasing

50g *(⅓ cup)* plain *(all-purpose)* flour, sifted

50g *(⅓ cup)* ground almonds

250g *(generous 2 cups)* icing *(confectioner's)* sugar

4 egg whites

½ teaspoon vanilla paste or extract

½ teaspoon almond oil or pure extract

Method

Preheat the oven to 190°C/375°F. Melt the 2 tablespoons butter and use to brush the insides of a financier mould or moulds (or you can use mini loaf tins, or tartlets tins).

Melt the 75g (⅓ cup) of butter and set aside to cool. Sift the flour and ground almonds into a large bowl, add the icing sugar and whisk to combine using a balloon whisk. In a separate bowl, whisk the egg whites just enough to break them up and make them a little frothy. Add these to the flour mixture with the melted butter, vanilla and almond oil and stir to combine. Pour the mixture into the prepared moulds or tins and bake for 15–20 minutes or until lightly golden.

Note: If you'd like to follow the original French recipe for using *beurre noisette* (brown butter), melt the butter for the cake mixture in a small saucepan as light in colour as possible (so you can see when the butter reaches the right stage). Let the butter melt and bubble, without stirring, but swirling the pan every so often. First you'll see foam creating on the surface, which will drop down and transform into bubbles. The milk solids will drop down the bottom of the pan leaving clarified butter on top. Continue to swirl the pan and you'll see the butter changing colour rapidly and start to brown. Be very careful at this stage to avoid burning and, as soon as it is brown, remove from the heat and pour into a bowl to cool to room temperature before continuing with the recipe as above. Discard the brown bits stuck to the bottom of the pan.

MELKTERT CROSTATA AL LATTE

MELKTERT MILK TART

There is a saying that once you have been to Africa you will go back to Africa... and it's true for me. I first visited a while ago and have never forgotten the places I went and the people I met. I also had some amazing food, of which this tart is a fine example. Melktert originally comes from South Africa, but you can find it in many other areas, and I ate it in Tanzania on a picnic in the wild Savannah, while watching the majestic nature around me. It's a simple, milky, smooth and comforting tart that you can eat chilled from the fridge if you prefer it dense, or at room temperature for a creamier feel. Whichever way, kids love it too!

Serves 8–10

Ingredients

For the pastry

120g (½ cup) butter, plus extra for greasing

120g (½ cup plus 2 tablespoons) caster (granulated) sugar

4 egg yolks

1 teaspoon vanilla paste or extract

280g (2 cups) plain (all-purpose) flour

For the filling

2 tablespoons cornflour (cornstarch)

2 tablespoons plain (all-purpose) flour

2 eggs

500ml (scant 2 cups) milk

100g (½ cup) caster (granulated) sugar

¼ teaspoon salt

1 teaspoon vanilla paste or extract

Good-quality cocoa powder, for dusting

Method

Butter a 23-cm/9-inch loose-based fluted tart tin.

For the pastry, beat the butter and sugar together in the bowl of a stand mixer or a mixing bowl and using electric hand-held beaters, until pale and fluffy. Beat in the egg yolks and vanilla. Add the flour and beat until incorporated. Using your hands, bring the dough together, wrap in cling film (plastic wrap) and refrigerate for 30 minutes.

Remove the dough from the fridge, and roll out to about 3mm/⅛ inch thick. Carefully place it into the tart tin. Press the pastry gently into the tin. Trim off any excess dough and put the tart back in the fridge for about 20 minutes. Meanwhile, preheat the oven to 180°C/350°F.

Remove the tart case from the fridge, line with parchment paper, fill with baking beans and blind bake for 15 minutes, until golden, checking during baking as you don't want it to brown too much. Remove from the oven and leave to cool.

Put the cornflour, plain flour and eggs into a bowl and, using a balloon whisk, whisk together.

Heat the milk, sugar and salt in a medium saucepan set over a medium heat, stirring continuously, until the sugar has completely dissolved. Bring to a gentle simmer, then remove from the heat and set aside to cool slightly.

When cooled but still warm, pour the milk mixture into the egg mixture, whisking with a balloon whisk to avoid lumps; it will thicken as you whisk. Once fully incorporated, return to the pan, add the vanilla and cook for a few more minutes until dense and creamy. Pour into the tart case and leave to cool at room temperature. Once cooled, refrigerate for at least 1 hour before serving, dusted with cocoa powder.

OLD-FASHIONED AMERICAN CAKE

I collect cookbooks. And those of you who do the same will probably know how much fun it is to search for antique publications, rare discoveries or lost books. Of course, baking is my passion, so my collection is well stocked... I unearthed this recipe for a buttery, yellow vanilla sponge topped with a quick, foolproof chocolate icing from a book dated 1850! I have brought it up to date just a little, and it's a hit at my bakery and tea room. Try it, and save it in your recipe notebook... because you do have one, right?

Serves 12–14

Ingredients

115g (½ cup) butter, at room temperature, plus extra for greasing

280g (2 cups) plain (all-purpose) flour

1 tablespoon baking powder

1 teaspoon salt

250ml (generous 1 cup) milk

1 vanilla pod (the best quality you can find)

250g (1¼ cups) caster (granulated) sugar

2 eggs

250g (9oz) dark chocolate chips, or dark chocolate cut into small chunks

Chocolate shavings, to decorate

For the icing

115g (½ cup) butter

80g (¾ cup) good-quality cocoa powder

490g (scant 5 cups) icing (confectioner's) sugar, sifted

60ml (¼ cup) milk

Method

Preheat the oven to 180°C/350°F. Butter two 20-cm/8-inch cake tins and line the bases with baking parchment.

Sift the flour into a bowl and add the baking powder and salt. Put the milk into a pan set over a medium heat. Cut the vanilla pod lengthways and scrape out the seeds, using the tip of a knife. Add the seeds to the milk, bring to a gentle simmer, then take off the heat, cover and leave to infuse.

Meanwhile, in the bowl of a stand mixer, or in a mixing bowl and using electric hand-held beaters, beat the butter and sugar together until fluffy. Beat in the eggs one at a time. Once incorporated, stir in the flour and warm milk alternately in three batches, starting and ending with the flour and using a spatula. Finally, stir in the chocolate chips using the spatula. Divide the mixture evenly between the prepared tins and bake in the oven for 20–25 minutes, until a skewer inserted in the middle comes out clean. Remove from the oven before inverting on to a wire rack to cool.

For the icing, melt the butter in a microwave or in a small pan set over a low heat. Put the melted butter and cocoa powder into the bowl of a stand mixer, or into a mixing bowl and using electric hand-held beaters, and beat on a low speed. Gradually add the icing sugar and milk alternately, in small additions. Depending on temperature and humidity, you might need to add more or less milk – you are looking for a spreadable buttercream consistency. If the icing is a little loose, refrigerate it for 15 minutes and stir before using.

To assemble, place a cooled cake on a plate. Spread plenty of icing over and top with the second cake. Cover the entire cake with the remaining icing. Refrigerate for at least 30 minutes before serving, topped with chocolate shavings.

SABLÉS BRETONS

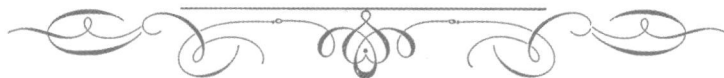

This is a tribute to my dear French friend G, who comes from Brittany. We shared some tough years and adventures together, renting tiny bedsits in London when we were very young and broke. I remember him talking over and over about all the beauties of his country, about *la chanson française*, the wonderful wine, and how much he missed home. We kept each other company during lonely, rainy winter nights, talking for hours and listening to music, while eating *sablé breton* and drinking French wine. Life felt so complicated and difficult. I didn't know it at the time, but those were the best years of my life. Thank you, G

Makes about 18–20

Ingredients

70g (*⅓ cup*) **caster (*granulated*) sugar**

1 teaspoon *fleur de sel* (or other flaky sea salt)

2 egg yolks

1 teaspoon vanilla paste or extract, or the seeds of 1 vanilla pod

80g (*generous ⅓ cup*) butter, softened

100g (*¾ cup plus 1 tablespoon*) plain (*all-purpose*) flour

1 teaspoon baking powder

For the egg wash

2 egg yolks mixed with 1 teaspoon milk

Method

In the bowl of a stand mixer, or in a mixing bowl and using electric hand-held beaters, beat the sugar, salt, egg yolks and vanilla to a homogeneous consistency. Add the softened butter and beat until fully incorporated.

Sift the flour and baking powder together, add to the bowl and beat with the beaters on a low speed, or with a wooden spoon, until combined. Remove the dough to a large sheet of baking parchment on the work surface, place a second sheet of parchment on top and roll dough out as thinly as possible between the sheets. Put in the fridge until firm (at least 30 minutes).

Preheat the oven to 190°C/375°F.

Remove the dough from the fridge and peel off the top sheet of baking parchment. Brush egg wash over the surface of the dough, then run the tips of a fork to make parallel lines over the surface, then across again, to create the characteristic *sablé breton* criss-cross pattern.

Carefully transfer the dough on its parchment to a baking sheet, and part-bake in the oven for 5–7 minutes. Remove from the oven and, using a round, medium cookie cutter, cut out circles, leaving the excess dough in between the rounds. Bake for 10 more minutes until golden, then remove from the oven. Leave to cool on the baking sheet for 5 minutes before transferring the cookies to a wire rack to cool completely.

TORTA DI NANTES

NANTES CAKE

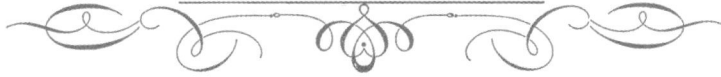

The world is truly a wonderful place, and Nantes, a port in western France, is no exception. The city is a perfect balance between heritage and innovation, with very kind and warm people as well. If you haven't been, do consider a visit. The city has also gifted us with this rich rum and almond gâteau. Because of its position, Nantes was among the first places in Europe to receive rum exported from Martinique, and this cake is a perfect blend of French rustic tradition and exotic flavours.

Being a very curious Italian, travelling is such an important part of life to me, and although I am lucky to have travelled quite a bit, there are still many places I wish to explore. My mission? To bring home a suitcase full of amazing recipes from each of the countries I have visited. In part, this is what this book is about, and in a large part this is what my work and my shop are about too. This cake tastes even better one or two days after it is made.

Serves 6–8

Ingredients

115g (½ cup) butter, softened (see Note), plus extra for greasing

3 tablespoons plain (all-purpose) flour, plus extra for dusting

125g (½ cup plus 2 tablespoons) caster (granulated) sugar

115g (¾ cup) ground almonds

1½ teaspoons baking powder

100ml (scant ½ cup) light or dark rum

3 eggs, lightly beaten

3 tablespoons apricot jam

100g (⅔ cup) icing (confectioner's) sugar

Method

Preheat the oven to 180°C/350°F. Butter a 20-cm/8-inch cake tin and dust with flour.

Place the butter and sugar in a large bowl and, using a balloon whisk, work the ingredients until creamy and fluffy. Add the flour, ground almonds and baking powder and continue to whisk. Add half the rum, and finally the eggs. Whisk until fully incorporated.

Transfer the mixture to the prepared tin and bake for about 40 minutes until a skewer inserted in the middle comes out clean, and the edges of the cake are golden. Leave the cake to cool for 5 minutes before inverting on to a baking sheet lined with baking parchment.

While the cake is cooling a little, warm the apricot jam in a small bowl in the microwave for just a few seconds. Strain through a sieve and brush it over the still-warm cake, using a pastry brush.

Put the icing sugar and the remaining rum into a separate bowl and stir until fully blended and resembling a thick royal icing. Pour this over the cake, either letting it drip down the sides, or spreading it evenly over the surface. Set aside at room temperature until the royal icing has set. Once set, place it in the fridge until ready to serve.

Note: The butter needs to be very soft (the French call it *beurre pommade*), so leave the butter on your kitchen counter overnight before using it. If you don't have time for this, or your kitchen is cold, then carefully soften the butter in the microwave, taking great care not to let it melt.

TORTA TIRAMISÙ A MODO MIO

TIRAMISÙ CAKE MY WAY

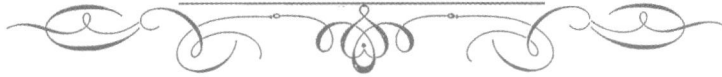

"Lift me up"! This is what tiramisù means literally. There are many versions of this dessert, some following the traditional way of using *savoiardi* sponge biscuits (cookies), others just consisting of mascarpone cream poured into a glass or ramekin and dusted with cocoa powder. In Liguria, where I live, they use a type of light, sweet cookie called a *pavesino*. This is yet another version of the dessert, prepared my way. At my shop this cake sells really, really fast and I am sure it will disappear pretty quickly in your house too! Serve it at the end of a dinner, or have it for breakfast, or simply whenever you feel down or tired and need to be "lifted up"!

Serves 8–12

Ingredients

A little softened butter, for greasing

285g (*2 cups plus 2 tablespoons*) plain (*all-purpose*) flour

1½ teaspoons baking powder

200g (*1 cup*) caster (*superfine*) sugar

4 eggs, separated

¼ teaspoon cream of tartar

100ml (*scant ½ cup*) vegetable oil

200ml (*¾ cup plus 1 tablespoon*) strong brewed black coffee

A pinch of salt

1 teaspoon vanilla paste or extract

Good-quality cocoa powder, for dusting

For the mascarpone frosting

250ml (*1 cup plus 2 teaspoons*) double (*heavy*) cream

250g (*9oz*) mascarpone cheese

90g (*½ cup plus 1 tablespoon*) icing (*confectioner's*) sugar

Method

Preheat the oven to 180°C/350°F. Butter two 20-cm/8-inch cake tins and line the bases with baking parchment.

Sift the flour into a medium bowl, add the baking powder and half the sugar and whisk to combine.

Put the egg yolks into the bowl of a stand mixer fitted with a paddle attachment and place the egg whites in a large, clean bowl with the cream of tartar. Add the oil, half the coffee, the salt and vanilla to the egg yolks and beat until mixed, then add the flour mixture and beat until well incorporated; do not over-mix.

Using an electric hand-held whisk, whisk the egg whites until frothy, then add the remaining sugar and whisk to stiff peaks. Gently fold the whisked egg whites into the cake mixture, then divide the mixture between the prepared tins and bake for 20–25 minutes, until a skewer inserted in the middle comes out clean. Remove the cakes from the oven and brush of the remaining coffee over both, using a pastry brush. Wait for it to soak in, about 2 minutes, then invert the cakes on to a wire rack and cool.

For the mascarpone frosting, whip the cream in a mixing bowl, using an electric hand-held whisk, until medium stiff. Meanwhile using the paddle attachment on the stand mixer, beat the mascarpone until creamy. Beat the whipped cream into the mascarpone and icing sugar.

To assemble, brush the remaining coffee over both cooled cakes. Place one cake on a cake board or plate. Spread some mascarpone cream over the top, using a spatula. Dust generously with cocoa powder and top with the second cake. Spread the remaining mascarpone cream over the top and sides of the cake. Dust the top with cocoa powder.

CHAMPAGNE CAKE

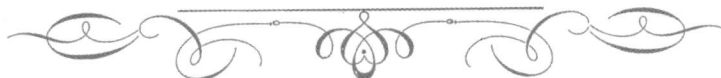

Nothing is more festive than Champagne – that's a fact – and serving a Champagne cake is a great way to double the bubbles. So if you have any leftover New Year's Eve Champagne, which I strongly doubt, or you simply want a fun, chic cake, then look no further. This is for you.

Serves 10–12

Ingredients

100ml (*⅓ cup plus 1½ tablespoons*) vegetable oil (ideally organic sunflower), plus extra for greasing

4 egg whites, at room temperature

225g (*1½ cups*) caster (*granulated*) sugar

280g (*2 cups*) plain (*all-purpose*) flour, sifted

3 teaspoons baking powder

1 teaspoon salt

245ml (*1 cup*) Champagne, at room temperature

2 tablespoons double (*heavy*) cream

1½ teaspoons vanilla paste or extract

For the filling and frosting

500ml (*2 cups plus 2 tablespoons*) double (*heavy*) cream

2 tablespoons icing (*confectioner's*) sugar

80g (*3oz*) good-quality strawberry jam

Method

Preheat the oven to 180°C/350°F. Lightly oil two 20-cm/8-inch cake tins and line the bases and sides with baking parchment.

In a stand mixer fitted with the whisk attachment (or in a mixing bowl and using a hand-held electric whisk) whisk the egg whites until frothy, then whisk in 100g (½ cup) of the sugar in small additions, whisking until stiff peaks form and the meringue looks glossy.

Put the flour, baking powder, remaining sugar and salt in a separate bowl. Add the vegetable oil, Champagne, cream and vanilla. Beat until incorporated, then gently fold in the whisked egg whites. Divide the batter between the prepared tins and bake for 30 minutes until a skewer inserted in the middle comes out clean. Leave to cool in the tins for 10 minutes before inverting on to a wire rack to cool completely.

In the meantime, place a stand mixer or a mixing bowl in the freezer for 15–20 minutes to chill. Using the whisk attachment or a hand-held electric whisk, whisk the double cream and icing sugar together in the chilled bowl, until it reaches a spreadable consistency.

To assemble, spread a thin layer of jam over one cake and top with whipped cream. Place the other cake over the first and, using a spatula, spread the whipped cream evenly over the top and sides.

Note: If you'd like a pink cake, add a drop or two of strawberry or raspberry purée to the whipped cream.

SHORTBREAD ARANCIA E CIOCCOLATO

ORANGE AND CHOCOLATE SHORTBREAD COOKIES

My favourite deli when I was growing up in Rome was called Castroni, which still exists today and is famous for displaying ingredients and products from all over the world. I used to go there with my father to buy freshly ground coffee and, while my dad was busy choosing the best beans from South America, I would browse the aisles looking at exotic packaging and colourful labels: syrups from the States, chocolates from Belgium, maple candies from Canada and shortbread cookies from Scotland! These last ones came in tins or boxes decorated in tartan motifs and it was love at first sight! I managed to convince my father to buy me a box and, once home, I went into my room and served shortbread and tea on my vintage toy tea set. The guest of honour? Her Majesty the Queen of course!

This is a variation of a classic and will smell wonderful on your Christmas table. You can also hang them on the Christmas tree or wrap them as presents for friends and family.

Makes 15–20, depending on size

Ingredients

230g *(1 cup)* butter,
  at room temperature

Finely grated zest of 1 orange

1 teaspoon vanilla paste
  or extract

80g *(2/3 cup)* icing
  (confectioner's) sugar

280g *(2 cups)* plain
  (all-purpose) flour,
  plus extra for dusting

180g *(6oz)* dark chocolate,
  finely chopped

Method

In the bowl of a stand mixer, or in a mixing bowl and using electric hand-held beaters, beat the butter just enough for it to reach a smooth consistency, without incorporating too much air. Beat in the orange zest and vanilla. Add the icing sugar and beat until combined. Finally, add the flour and beat until incorporated. Transfer the mixture to the work surface and bring together with your hands to form a dough. Flatten into a thick disc, wrap in cling film (plastic wrap) and refrigerate for at least 1 hour, or better still overnight.

Preheat the oven to 180°C/350°F. Line a baking sheet with baking parchment.

Roll out the chilled dough on a lightly floured surface to 4mm/⅛ inch thick and, using a cutter of your choice, stamp out cookies and place them on the lined baking sheet. Bake for about 10–15 minutes until pale golden brown.

Leave to cool on the baking sheet. Meanwhile, put half the chocolate in a bowl set over barely simmering water, making sure the bowl is not touching the water, and allow to melt. Once melted, add the remaining chocolate and stir until melted and smooth.

Take one cooled cookie, dip one half into the melted chocolate and transfer to a tray lined with a sheet of baking parchment. Repeat with the remaining cookies. Transfer to the fridge for the chocolate to set, then bring the cookies to room temperature to serve.

JUMBO MUFFINS ARANCIA CARDAMOMO E SEMI DI PAPAVERO

JUMBO ORANGE, CARDAMOM AND POPPY SEED MUFFINS

I spent a long time searching for a good and reliable muffin recipe, and after years of "muffin testing" I came up with this, which has since worked perfectly as a base for hundreds of different combinations. It calls for buttermilk, and because this is almost impossible to find in Italy, I make my own (see Note). These muffins are best eaten on the day they are made, but popping them in the microwave for 10 seconds will bring them back to life.

Makes 6

Ingredients

65ml (*generous ¼ cup*) vegetable oil, plus extra for greasing (optional)

300g (*scant 2½ cups*) plain (*all-purpose*) flour

3 teaspoons baking powder

1 teaspoon ground cardamom

4 tablespoons poppy seeds

100g (*½ cup*) caster (*granulated*) sugar

50g (*¼ cup*) brown sugar

250ml (*generous 1 cup*) buttermilk

3 eggs

1 teaspoon vanilla paste or extract

Grated zest and juice of 2 oranges

Method

Preheat the oven to 180°C/350°F. Using your fingers, rub oil into 6 cavities of a muffin tray. (Alternatively, fill the tray with paper cases.)

Put all the dry ingredients into a bowl and stir to combine using a wooden spoon. Put the oil, buttermilk, eggs, vanilla and orange zest and juice into a jug or another bowl. Whisk to combine, then add the wet ingredients to the dry ingredients and, using a wooden spoon or spatula, fold to just combine. Do not over-mix (this is very important as over-mixing results in tough muffins) – there should be visible streaks of flour.

Fill the oiled cavities or paper cases with the mixture, to come almost to the top, and bake for about 25 minutes, until nicely risen and cooked through.

Note: To make your own buttermilk, add 1 tablespoon white wine vinegar or lemon juice to every 250ml/cup of milk. Cover and leave to stand for 10 minutes.

TARTUFI AL COINTREAU

COINTREAU CHOCOLATE TRUFFLES

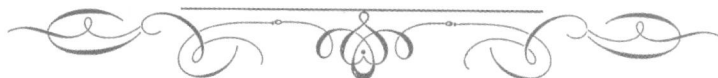

Making truffles is another of my fond childhood memories. It was a serious matter in my house and the whole ritual was very messy! Of course, Cointreau was off limits for me when I was little, but boozy truffles are always very welcome among grown-ups. With a little organization you can make truffles with your kids – and have great fun too – using orange juice in place of the Cointreau, or leaving them plain. They work well as an edible Christmas gift for friends and family, presented in small paper cases, in a fancy box wrapped with an elegant ribbon. *Et voilà*!

Makes about 24, depending on size

Ingredients

225g *(8oz)* good-quality dark chocolate (60% cocoa solids)

115ml *(½ cup)* double *(heavy)* cream

1 tablespoon butter

2 tablespoons Cointreau liqueur

Good-quality cocoa powder, for coating

Method

Finely grate the chocolate using a cheese grater, or chop it very finely, and put it in a large heatproof bowl. Set aside.

Bring the cream to a gentle boil in a saucepan set over a medium heat, then pour it over the chocolate. Leave to stand for 1 minute then gently start stirring, using a metal spoon. Add the butter and stir a little more, making sure the chocolate is completely melted. Finally, add the Cointreau and stir to combine. Cover the bowl with cling film (plastic wrap) and refrigerate for at least a couple of hours or, better still, overnight.

Using a teaspoon or a small scoop, form the mixture into small balls. Making sure your hands are cool (wash in cold water and dry well, if not), roll each ball in the sifted cocoa powder.

Shake the excess cocoa gently from each and place the truffles on a sheet of baking parchment to set. Leave to stand at room temperature until completely solid. In warm weather, store them in the fridge until ready to serve.

TORTA VALENCIA

VALENCIA ORANGE CAKE (GLUTEN-FREE)

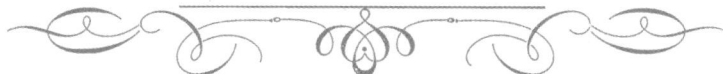

Valencia oranges are truly something spectacular. Of course you can make this cake using other varieties, but if you can find Valencia you'll be true to the recipe, and will taste the sun that this fruit holds within. As you will use the zest, I strongly urge you to use organic, whichever variety of orange you find.

I am so lucky to be able to buy organic fruit and vegetables from a farm just down the road from my house; I can't tell you what pleasure it is for me to go to there. The fruit and vegetables are picked fresh every morning and sometimes I'm even allowed me to choose what I want straight from the crop: heaven! And you know something else? It's cheaper than buying from the supermarket. If you live in a big city, look for farms right outside the city – trust me, there are many in every country! A little effort and life will be better for us all.

Serves 8–12

Ingredients

3 Valencia oranges

200g *(1 cup)* light brown sugar

4 eggs

1 teaspoon honey

Grated zest of 2 oranges

300g *(3 cups)* ground almonds

1 teaspoon baking powder

For the orange syrup

1 large Valencia orange

150g *(¾ cup)* caster *(granulated)* sugar

Method

Grease a 23-cm/9-inch springform cake tin and line the base with baking parchment.

For the syrup, squeeze the juice from the orange and pour into a small saucepan. Place over a low to medium heat, add the sugar and heat gently, without stirring, until the sugar is completely dissolved. Remove from the heat and leave to cool while you make the cake.

Peel the oranges and remove the pith, and seeds if there are any. Chop the flesh and place it in a saucepan. Cover with water and cook for about 20 minutes, then drain, transfer to a blender or food processor and pulse until smooth. Meanwhile, preheat the oven to 170°C/335°F.

Put the sugar, eggs and honey in a bowl and beat until pale (by hand or using electric hand-held beaters). Fold in the puréed orange and orange zest, then, using a spatula, gently fold in the ground almonds and baking powder. Pour the mixture into the prepared tin and bake for about 30 minutes, until a skewer inserted in the middle comes out clean.

Remove from the oven and pour the syrup all over the cake. Leave to cool in the tin for about 20 minutes before unmoulding. Cut into slices and serve with a dollop of crème fraîche if you like extra tanginess.

GENOISE MERINGATA E ARANCIA

ORANGE MERINGUE GENOISE

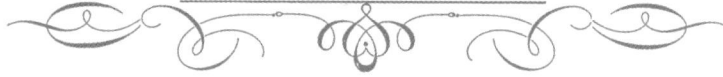

During my early days as a baker, genoise was the one preparation I was most scared of. Whenever there are very few ingredients in a recipe, I find things get complicated. So when technique is called for, you can never be blasé about following the recipe, and you'd be surprised how many times I have forgotten to add an ingredient because I was too sure of myself. Just follow the method carefully and you won't be disappointed. Gorgeous on a cake stand in the middle of the table...

Serves 10–12

Ingredients

For the orange filling

250g (1¼ cups) caster (granulated) sugar

1½ tablespoons cornflour (cornstarch)

¼ teaspoon salt

3 teaspoons finely grated orange zest

160ml (⅔ cup) freshly squeezed orange juice, strained

2 tablespoons lemon juice

1 whole egg plus 4 egg yolks

4 tablespoons butter, cut into small pieces

For the genoise

100g (⅓ cup plus 1½ tablespoons) butter, melted and cooled, plus extra for greasing

150g (1¼ cups) plain (all-purpose) flour, plus extra for dusting

4 eggs, at room temperature

100g (½ cup) caster (superfine) sugar

1 teaspoon vanilla paste or extract

For the meringue frosting

4 egg whites

¼ teaspoon cream of tartar

100g (½ cup) caster (superfine) sugar

Method

For the filling, put the sugar, cornflour and salt in a pan and whisk together. Stir in the orange zest and juice, and the lemon juice. Bring to a boil over a medium heat, stirring frequently, and boil for 1 minute. The mixture should thicken slightly and turn translucent. Remove from the heat.

Whisk the whole egg and yolks in a bowl, until blended. Slowly pour 60ml (¼ cup) of the hot orange juice mixture over the eggs and stir until well mixed. Stirring, slowly pour the egg mixture into the pan with the remaining orange mixture. Reduce the heat to medium-low and cook, whisking vigorously with a small balloon whisk, until thickened, about 4 minutes. Remove from the heat, add the butter and stir until combined. Pour into a bowl, lay cling film (plastic wrap) directly on the surface, and chill for 2 hours.

Preheat the oven to 180°C/350°F. Butter the bases and sides of two 18-cm/7-inch cake tins and dust with flour. In the bowl of a stand mixer, or in a mixing bowl (set over a pan of hot water) and using hand-held electric beaters, beat the eggs, sugar and vanilla together for about 5 minutes, until tripled in volume. Sift the flour twice and fold it very gently into the egg mixture. Pour the cooled melted butter into the mixture and fold again. Immediately divide the batter between the prepared tins and bake for about 30 minutes, until a skewer inserted in the middle comes out clean. Leave to cool in the tins for 10 minutes before inverting on to a wire rack to cool completely.

For the meringue frosting, put the egg whites and sugar into a very clean heatproof bowl and set it over a pan of barely simmering water. Stirring constantly, heat until it registers 160°C on a jam thermometer, about 3–5 minutes. Remove the bowl from the saucepan, add the cream of tartar and whisk the mixture in an electric stand mixer (or with an electric hand-held whisk) until stiff, glossy peaks form, about 7–9 minutes.

To assemble, spread half of the chilled orange filling over one cake, leaving a clean border, about 5mm/¼ inch. Place the second cake on top, followed by the remaining orange filling. Spread the meringue over the entire cake. Using a kitchen blowtorch, flame the meringue all over until lightly golden. Serve immediately or store, covered, in the fridge, and bring to room temperature before serving.

TORTA AL TÈ CHAI E ZENZERO

CHAI AND GINGER LAYER CAKE

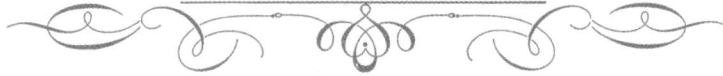

I am always in search of new combinations for creating cakes and desserts. Chai is one of my favourite teas – it holds a mysterious flavour created by an exotic blend of spices including cinnamon, cardamom, ginger, cloves and black peppercorns. A dash of milk adds an unexpected explosion of taste and a little honey enriches it even more. All these ingredients are in this cake. It makes me think of faraway lands and the wonderful aromas of Sri Lanka, where I visited some years ago. It's a sort of obsession of mine to translate into flavours the experiences that I don't want to forget. Our senses allow us to remember the past through food.

Serves 12–14

Ingredients

300g (1⅓ cups) butter, at room temperature, plus extra for greasing

245ml (1 cup) milk

6 Chai tea bags (the best you can find, ideally organic)

300g (1½ cups) caster (granulated) sugar

5 eggs

1 teaspoon vanilla paste or extract

350g (2¾ cups) plain (all-purpose) flour

3½ teaspoons baking powder

1 teaspoon ground cinnamon

½ teaspoon ground cardamom

½ teaspoon salt

For the frosting

200g (scant 1 cup) butter, softened

80g (3oz) acacia or other clear honey

500g (1lb 2oz) cream cheese

½ teaspoon freshly grated ginger

150g (1½ cups) icing (confectioner's) sugar, sifted

Method

Butter two 20-cm/8-inch cake tins and line the bases and sides with baking parchment.

In a small saucepan, bring the milk to a simmer over a low to medium heat. Add the tea bags, remove from the heat and allow to infuse for 5–8 minutes. Remove the teabags, squeezing them out into the milk. Leave the milk to cool completely.

Preheat the oven to 180°C/350°F. In the bowl of a stand mixer, or in a mixing bowl and using hand-held electric beaters, cream the butter and sugar together until fluffy. Add the eggs one at a time and beat until incorporated, then add the vanilla.

Sift the flour into a separate bowl and mix in the baking powder, cinnamon, cardamom and salt. Add the flour mixture and the cooled milk to the egg mixture alternately, in three additions, beating until well mixed but taking care not to over-mix.

Divide the mixture between the prepared tins and bake for about 40 minutes or until a skewer inserted in the middle comes out clean. Leave to cool in the tins for 10 minutes before inverting on to a wire rack to cool completely.

Meanwhile, prepare the frosting. In the bowl of a stand mixer, or in a mixing bowl and using electric hand-held beaters, beat the softened butter and honey together until creamy. Add the cream cheese and ginger and beat until incorporated. Finally add the icing sugar and beat just enough for the sugar to blend in. Refrigerate to set a little while the cakes are cooling.

To assemble, place one cake on a plate. Spread with about a quarter of the frosting and place the second cake on top. Spread the remaining frosting all over the top and sides of the cake. Create a wave pattern using the back of a spoon.

TORTA AL MATCHA E LAMPONI

MATCHA AND RASPBERRY CAKE

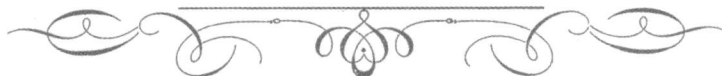

Matcha, a finely ground, vibrant green powder made from the leaves of a special type of green tea, is such an extraordinary ingredient; versatile and with a very particular flavour. And delicious paired with chocolate. At the tea room I use organic matcha powder and I suggest you do the same for this recipe; it's readily available these days, and you can use any you have left to brew some healthy tea!

Serves 8

Ingredients

100g (⅓ cup plus 1½ tablespoons) butter, plus extra for greasing

6 tablespoons milk, at room temperature

6 eggs, at room temperature

180g (¾ cup plus 2 tablespoons) caster (granulated) sugar

160g (just over 1¼ cups) plain (all-purpose) flour

4 teaspoons matcha powder, ideally organic

250g (9oz) raspberries, plus extra to decorate

For the frosting

250ml (1 cup plus 1 tablespoon) double (heavy) cream

Matcha powder, for dusting

Method

Preheat the oven to 160°C/320°F. Butter the insides of two 18-cm/7-inch cake tins and line the bases and sides with baking parchment.

In a small pan, warm the milk and butter until the butter is fully melted, then set aside to cool.

Crack the eggs into the bowl of a stand mixer (or into a mixing bowl and use an electric hand-held whisk) add the sugar and whisk for about 8 minutes, until very pale and tripled in volume.

Sift the flour and matcha powder together three times (to aerate), then add them to the egg mixture and gently fold them in, making sure you don't deflate the batter. Add the cooled butter and milk mixture and fold in gently, using a spatula. Divide the mixture between the prepared tins and bake for 30 minutes until a skewer inserted in the middle comes out clean.

Remove the tins from the oven and, before putting them on the counter, let them drop down onto the counter. Do this twice and this will help stop the cakes from shrinking. Leave to cool in the tins for 10 minutes before inverting both cakes on to a wire rack. Leave to cool completely.

To assemble, place one cake on a serving plate or board. Whisk the cream for the frosting until medium stiff, then spread over the first cake and top with the raspberries in an even layer (cutting them in half or leaving them whole). Place the second cake on top and spread whipped cream over the top and sides of the cake, using a spatula. Dust matcha powder generously over the top to completely cover it. Decorate with raspberries, and pipe a cream border around the edge, if you wish.

LOAF ALLA CANNELLA

CINNAMON LOAF

Imagine having to wake up on a rainy, cold winter's morning to go to work... and now imagine sitting at your breakfast table with a cup of coffee and a slice of sweet, spiced cinnamon loaf. All of a sudden, being awake and ready to go to work doesn't look so bad any more – that's the positive power of cinnamon! Strongly recommended for any time of day, it's a real mood booster.

Serves 8–10

Ingredients

For the cake

120g (*½ cup plus 1 teaspoon*) butter, at room temperature, plus extra for greasing

150g (*1¼ cups*) plain (*all-purpose*) flour

1½ teaspoons baking powder

¼ teaspoon bicarbonate of soda (*baking soda*)

180g (*¾ cup plus 2 tablespoons*) caster (*superfine*) sugar

2 eggs

2 teaspoons vanilla paste or extract

300ml (*1¼ cups*) buttermilk

For the spiced sugar

60g (*scant ⅓ cup*) demerara sugar, plus extra for sprinkling

60g (*scant ⅓ cup*) caster (*granulated*) sugar

1 tablespoon ground cinnamon

½ teaspoon ground nutmeg

¼ teaspoon ground aniseed (optional)

Method

Preheat the oven to 180°C/350°F. Butter the insides of a 1lb long loaf tin and sprinkle with brown sugar.

For the spiced sugar, put the brown sugar, caster sugar, cinnamon, nutmeg and aniseed, if using, in a bowl and mix together, using a balloon whisk. Cover and leave to stand for 10 minutes.

In a medium bowl, sift together the flour, baking powder and bicarbonate of soda and set aside. In the bowl of stand mixer, or using a mixing bowl and electric hand-held beaters, beat the butter and sugar together until light and fluffy. Beat in the eggs, one at a time, add the vanilla and continue beating. Finally, in three additions, stir in the flour mixture and the buttermilk alternately.

Spread some of the cake mixture into the base of the prepared loaf tin, then sprinkle some of the spiced sugar mixture over, then add a little more cake mixture followed by more spiced sugar, continuing the layers until you have used up all the ingredients, and ending with a layer of spiced sugar.

Bake in the oven for about 40–45 minutes until dark golden and caramelized, and leave to cool in the tin for 20 minutes before inverting on to a wire rack to cool completely.

A

COMPILATION

of recipes

DA MELISSA

from *my personal*

COOKBOOK

TORTA DI MELE DELLA ZIA ROSE

AUNT ROSE'S APPLE CAKE

I've eaten many, many apple cakes in my life. German strudel... love it! English apple pie... simply divine! But this fat-free recipe from my Aunt Rose is something totally different. Simple, healthy and so quick you will be able to make it in under an hour.

Serves 8

Ingredients

A little softened butter,
  for greasing

2 crisp dessert apples,
  such as Granny Smith

Finely grated zest and juice
  of 1 lemon

220g (2 cups) plain
  (all-purpose) flour, sifted

3 teaspoons baking powder

3 eggs

150g (¾ cup) caster
  (granulated) sugar,
  plus extra for sprinkling

1 teaspoon vanilla paste
  or extract

1 tablespoon Calvados

160ml (⅔ cup) good-quality
  ready-made vanilla custard
  (or homemade if you have
  time for it)

Method

Preheat the oven to 160°C/320°F. Butter the base and sides of a 23-cm/9-inch springform cake tin and line the base with baking parchment.

Peel and core the apples, then cut into thin segments. Put the slices in a bowl or dish, add the lemon juice and toss to coat (this will stop them turning brown while you make the cake); set aside.

Sift the flour into a bowl and add the baking powder. In the bowl of a stand mixer (or in a mixing bowl using hand-held electric beaters) beat the eggs, sugar, vanilla and lemon zest together until pale and fluffy, then add the Calvados.

Now add the dry ingredients and stir gently to combine. Pour the mixture into the prepared tin and pour the custard on top. Spread the apple slices on top of the custard, sprinkle with caster sugar and bake in the oven for 40 minutes, until golden and caramelized. Leave to cool in the tin.

TORTA DI RISO E CIOCCOLATO

RICE AND CHOCOLATE CAKE

In Italy there are many variations of rice cake and, from north to south, many regions claim to make the best version. Rice was once an ingredient widely used among poor people, which is why so many traditional recipes use this versatile grain. The cake I present to you here is inspired by the one made in the Emilia Romagna region. I have left out the candied fruits and added chocolate, for a more sinful twist. I hope you won't mind…

Serves 6–8

Ingredients

A little softened butter, for greasing

Good-quality cocoa powder, for dusting

2 oranges

1 litre *(scant 4 cups)* milk

1 vanilla pod, split in half lengthways and seeds scraped out

85g *(⅓ cup plus 1 tablespoon)* caster *(granulated)* sugar

300g *(11oz)* Arborio rice

4 eggs, separated

2 tablespoons Cointreau

60g *(2oz)* dark chocolate chips, or dark chocolate cut into chunks

Method

Butter a 20-cm/8-inch springform cake tin and dust with cocoa powder. Using a swivel peeler, pare the zest from one of the oranges into wide strips. Finely grate the zest from the other orange, keeping both zests separate.

Put the milk, vanilla seeds, sugar and the pared orange zest strips in a pan over a medium heat and stir to combine. Bring the mixture to a gentle simmer, then add the rice. Stir, cover and cook for 40 minutes, stirring occasionally, until the rice is cooked and the milk has all been absorbed. Transfer to a bowl and leave to cool. Remove and discard the pared orange zest.

Preheat the oven to 180°C/350°F. Beat the egg yolks in a bowl, using a whisk. Add half the Cointreau to the yolks.

In the bowl of a stand mixer fitted with a whisk attachment, or in a mixing bowl and using a hand-held electric whisk, whisk the eggs whites to stiff peaks. When the rice is cool to the touch, stir three quarters of the grated orange zest (or all of it if you don't want to reserve any for decoration at the end), the egg-yolk mixture and the remaining Cointreau into it.

Gently fold in the whisked egg whites until fully incorporated, then fold in the chocolate chips. Pour the mixture into the prepared tin and bake for 50–60 minutes until a skewer inserted in the middle comes out clean.

Leave to cool in the tin for 30 minutes before unmoulding on to a wire rack to cool completely. Dust generously with cocoa powder, sprinkle the remaining grated orange zest over the top, if you like, and serve.

CIAMBELLA CON CREMA ALLO ZABAIONE

CAKE WITH ZABAIONE CREAM

I came up with this recipe while leafing through an old culinary book I found in an antiques market. The recipe talked about an Italian cake made in the Lombardy region but did not give its name. The text of the recipe was not clear and time had faded the type, so the method was very hard to understand. But, curious for all things old and antique, I decided to give it a try. Here is my version, using clarified butter because it gives a fluffier texture and is rich in vitamins A, D and E. The addition of the Italian classic *zabaione*, a dense cream made with egg yolks and Marsala, creates a match made in heaven. This cake is absolutely perfect as a teatime treat or an after-dinner sin!

Serves 10–12

Ingredients

A little softened butter, for greasing

300g *(scant 2½ cups)* plain *(all-purpose)* flour, plus extra for dusting

A pinch of salt

1 tablespoon baking powder

130g *(½ cup)* clarified butter or ghee, melted

350g *(1¾ cups)* caster *(granulated)* sugar

4 eggs, separated

1 teaspoon vanilla paste or extract

1 tablespoon Maraschino cherry liqueur

1¼ teaspoons cream of tartar

150ml *(½ cup plus 2 tablespoons)* water, at room temperature

For the zabaione cream
8 egg yolks

160g *(¾ cup plus 2 teaspoons)* caster *(granulated)* sugar

100ml *(scant ½ cup)* Marsala (or Port or Madeira)

Method

Preheat the oven to 180°C/350°F. Butter a 23-cm/9-inch ring mould and dust with flour.

Sift the flour, salt and baking powder together and set aside. In the bowl of a stand mixer, or in a mixing bowl and using hand-held electric beaters, beat the melted clarified butter and sugar together until creamy. Add the egg yolks and continue beating, then add the vanilla and Maraschino.

In a separate bowl, whisk the egg whites until frothy. Add the cream of tartar and whisk until stiff peaks form. Gently fold the egg whites into the egg and butter mixture, until fully combined. Finally, fold in the sifted flour mixture in two additions. Pour the mixture into the ring mould, gently level the surface using a spatula and bake in the oven for about 35 minutes, until a skewer inserted in the middle comes out clean. Leave to cool completely before unmoulding.

To make the zabaione cream, put the egg yolks and sugar into a heatproof bowl. Using electric hand-held beaters or whisks, whisk until pale and doubled in size. Gradually whisk in the Marsala. Place the bowl over a pan of barely simmering water over a low heat, making sure the base of the bowl is not touching the water. Keep whisking over the pan until the cream becomes dense, rich and velvety. Transfer the cream to a bowl and leave to cool.

Serve slices of cake with a dollop of zabaione cream. You can store any leftover zabaione in the fridge for 2 days.

TORTA ALLE PESCHE E CREMA

PEACHES AND CREAM CAKE

This summer cake is delicious. When I was a teenager I used to go to my best friend's house and study for our end-of-year school exams. Or at least we used to pretend to study, while we listened to music all afternoon and talked about boys and make-up. Ah, well, all part of being a teenager I guess... My friend's grandma was famous for being an excellent home baker. She would make this cake saying: "You need energy to study! You must have a piece of cake!" Well, that was the sweetest sacrifice I ever had to make, I can tell you! Baking is about holding onto memories, so every time I make this cake, I think about that lovely woman... a real Italian, caring *nonna*!

Serves 8

Ingredients

125g (*generous ½ cup*) butter, melted, plus extra, softened, for greasing

200g (*1½ cups plus 2 tablespoons*) plain (*all-purpose*) flour, sifted, plus extra for dusting

3 large peaches

240ml (*1 cup*) water

1 cinnamon stick

½ star anise

130g (*⅔ cup*) granulated sugar

2 teaspoons baking powder

3 eggs

1 teaspoon vanilla paste or extract

1 quantity crème pâtissière from the chantilly cream in the Mimosa Cake on page 22, but omitting the double (*heavy*) cream

Icing (*confectioner's*) sugar, for dusting (optional)

Method

Preheat the oven to 190°C/375°F. Butter the base and sides of a 23-cm/9-inch springform cake tin and dust with flour.

Halve the peaches, remove the stone and cut into slices. Put the water, cinnamon, star anise and 1 tablespoon of the granulated sugar into a saucepan and bring to a boil over a medium heat. Add the peach slices and cook until tender then strain, reserving the syrup, and set aside to cool slightly.

Meanwhile, for the cake, sift the flour into a bowl and add the baking powder. In the bowl of stand mixer fitted with the whisk attachment (or use a mixing bowl and a hand-held electric whisk), whisk the eggs, the remaining sugar and the vanilla together until at least doubled in volume. Add the melted butter and continue to whisk until very pale and frothy. Finally, stir in the sifted flour.

Pour the batter into the prepared tin, spread a generous amount of crème pâtissière over the entire surface and arrange the peaches over the crème in a sunburst pattern. Bake for about 20 minutes, until the peaches are starting to caramelize and the cake is dark golden and cooked around the edges.

Leave to cool in the tin before inverting on to a plate. Serve in slices, with a dusting of icing sugar if you wish.

CROSTATA DI MARRON GLACÉ

MARRON GLACÉ TART

Very few things remind me of winter like chestnuts do. During Christmas in Rome, you see chestnut vendors everywhere, with their huge portable barbecues, wrapping the roasted wonders in paper to sell. Walking around the city eating them, with their aroma all around, looking at decorated Christmas trees in every square, kids singing carols on church corners, Piazza Navona with its market and lights, and a glass of mulled wine in one of the cafés around, is quintessential Roman Christmas for me. Many cafés serve chestnut cake of all kinds, but the one I truly adore is this tart. I tried it a long time ago in the famous Caffè Greco, off the Spanish Steps, and since then it has become one of my all-time favourite Christmas treats. You can decorate it with holly, glazed cranberries or simply leave it as it is.

Serves 8–10

Ingredients

For the pastry

350g (2¼ cups) plain (all-purpose) flour, plus extra for dusting

150g (¾ cup) caster (granulated) sugar

80g (generous ⅓ cup) butter, chilled and diced, plus extra, softened, for greasing

1 egg

1 teaspoon vanilla paste or extract

For the filling

350g (12oz) marron glacé purée

100g (½ cup) caster (granulated) sugar

300ml (1¼ cups) milk

250g (9oz) good-quality dark chocolate, chopped

4 tablespoons mascarpone cheese

Method

To make the pastry, process the flour, sugar and butter together in a food processor until the mixture resembles fine breadcrumbs. Add the egg and vanilla and process until the dough comes together. Turn the dough out onto a lightly floured surface and knead briefly until smooth, adding 1 tablespoon cold water if it doesn't come together easily. Shape into a disc, wrap in cling film (plastic wrap) and refrigerate for at least 40 minutes.

Meanwhile, for the filling, put the marron glacé purée in a saucepan over a medium heat and add the sugar and milk. Cook, stirring occasionally, for about 10 minutes. Add the chopped chocolate, remove from the heat and stir to melt. Once melted, leave to cool until warm to the touch, then stir in the mascarpone.

Preheat the oven to 170°C/335°F. Butter the insides of a 23-cm/9-inch fluted tart tin with a removable base, and dust with flour.

Roll out the chilled pastry to about a 3mm/⅛ inch thickness and use to line the prepared tin. Remove any excess dough overhanging the edges and place back in the fridge for 10–15 minutes to chill. Remove from the fridge and pour the cooled filling into the pastry case. Bake for 30 minutes or until the pastry is golden. Leave to cool before releasing the tart from the tin and cutting into slices to serve.

FROLLINI MONTATI

WHIPPED COOKIES

Nowadays, it is hard to find time to sit at the table in the morning and have a proper breakfast. Most of us Italians have a quick espresso and a croissant at a coffee bar on our way to work, and only on a Sunday morning do we find the time to enjoy breakfast at home. The first meal of the day usually consists of sweet pastries and sometimes a piece of focaccia. I usually have cookies for breakfast... yes, espresso and a couple of cookies. These ones in particular are very delicious – for breakfast, but also in the afternoon with a cup of tea.

Makes about 30

Ingredients

170g *(scant ¾ cup)* butter, at room temperature

150g *(1¼ cups)* icing *(confectioner's)* sugar

2 eggs

Finely grated zest of 1 lemon

1 teaspoon vanilla paste or extract

¼ teaspoon salt

340g *(2¾ cups)* plain *(all-purpose)* flour

Method

Line a baking sheet with baking parchment.

In the bowl of a stand mixer, or using a mixing bowl and electric hand-held beaters, beat the butter until creamy. Add the icing sugar and beat until fluffy. Add the eggs, lemon zest, vanilla and salt and beat until mixed. Finally, add the flour and beat until fully incorporated, but don't over-mix.

Fill a piping bag fitted with a large star-shaped nozzle with the mixture. Pipe rosettes of mixture onto the prepared sheet, leaving space between each cookie. Refrigerate for 20 minutes and preheat the oven to 170°C/335°F.

Bake in the oven for 10 minutes, until golden. Leave to cool on the baking sheet.

STUFATO ALLE MELE

APPLE CRUMBLE

For a last-minute dinner party, when craving comfort food and you are short of time but still want to impress your guests, then this recipe is for you. It will look as though you have spent hours in the kitchen baking, and your friends will be most impressed and grateful. Only you and I know how easy this recipe really is…

Serves 4

Ingredients

200g *(scant 1 cup)* butter, chilled and diced, plus extra, softened, for greasing

5 Reinette *(Gray Pippin)*, Cox or Gala apples

70g *(⅓ cup)* caster *(granulated)* sugar

50g *(2oz)* ground almonds

50g *(2oz)* raisins

150g *(1¼ cups)* plain *(all-purpose)* flour

50g *(¼ cup)* brown sugar

1 teaspoon ground cinnamon

Method

Preheat the oven to 180°/350°F. Butter a round baking or pie dish and set aside.

Peel and core the apples, then cut into chunks. Place in the baking dish and sprinkle over 1 tablespoon of the caster sugar, the ground almonds and the raisins.

Put the flour, remaining caster sugar and brown sugar, cinnamon and diced butter in a bowl and rub in the butter with your fingertips until the mixture resembles breadcrumbs. Spread the crumble evenly over the apples and bake for 40 minutes, until lightly golden and bubbling. Serve warm with or without custard.

TORTA DI GRANO SARACENO

BUCKWHEAT CAKE

Buckwheat is not, as its name suggests, a type of wheat, but a highly nutritional plant related to rhubarb. It finds a wide range of uses in the kitchen, and in Italy it is found in traditional recipes from the north, especially the Alps. This easy-to-make cake is typically a "cake from the mountains" and in Italy is eaten for breakfast, tea or as a snack.

Serves 8

Ingredients

100g (*⅓ cup plus 1½ tablespoons*) butter, melted, plus extra for greasing

150g (*1¼ cups*) plain (*all-purpose*) flour, sifted, plus extra for dusting

100g (*⅔ cup*) buckwheat flour

2 teaspoons baking powder

6 eggs

300g (*1½ cups*) caster (*granulated*) sugar

150g (*1½ cups*) mixed nuts, such as hazelnuts, pine nuts and walnuts

Finely grated zest of 1 lemon

100g (*⅓ cup*) wild blueberry jam

Icing (*confectioner's*) sugar, for dusting

Toasted hazelnuts, flaked (*slivered*) almonds and blueberries, to decorate (optional)

Method

Preheat the oven to 170°C/335°F. Butter the base and sides of a 20-cm/8-inch, deep cake tin and lightly dust with flour.

Sift both flours and baking powder into a bowl and set aside.

In the bowl of a stand mixer, or using a separate mixing bowl and electric hand-held beaters, beat the eggs and sugar together until pale. Gently fold in the flours with a spoon or spatula. Add the melted butter and nuts and fold in to incorporate. Finally, fold in the lemon zest.

Pour the batter into the prepared tin and bake for 35–40 minutes, until a skewer inserted into the centre comes out clean. Leave to cool in the tin for about 10 minutes before inverting on to a wire rack. Leave until cool to the touch. Cut the cake across into two layers, spread the jam over one layer and top with second layer. Dust with icing sugar, decorate with nuts and blueberries, if you like, then cut into slices and serve.

Note: Try giving your kids this as a healthy snack to take to school instead of processed food.

TORTA ALLO YOGURT

YOGURT SHEET CAKE

In Italy we don't have bake sales at school, but what we do have are end-of-term parties, where parents cook or, if lacking time, buy food for the kids to bring to school. My mum, although she hates cooking, used to prepare this simple sheet cake (or tray bake) for me to take in. Thank you, Mum, I know there was so much love in every cake you baked! Now it's my turn to bake for you.

Makes 16 squares

Ingredients

230g *(1 cup)* butter, at room temperature, plus extra for greasing

420g *(3 cups)* plain *(all-purpose)* flour, plus extra for dusting

2 teaspoons baking powder

1 teaspoon bicarbonate of soda *(baking soda)*

1 teaspoon salt

400g *(2 cups)* caster *(granulated)* sugar

2 teaspoons vanilla paste or extract

4 eggs

500g *(1lb 2oz)* full-fat plain yogurt

For the icing

380g *(generous 3 cups)* icing *(confectioner's)* sugar

3 tablespoons light corn syrup (or golden syrup)

115ml *(scant ½ cup)* double *(heavy)* cream

1 teaspoon vanilla paste or extract

Method

Preheat the oven to 180°C/350°F. Butter a 25-cm/10-inch square baking tin and line the base with baking parchment. Dust the inside with a little flour, tapping off the excess.

In a bowl, sift together the flour, baking powder, bicarbonate of soda and salt.

In the bowl of a stand mixer, or in a mixing bowl and using electric hand-held beaters, beat the butter, sugar and vanilla together until pale and fluffy. Beat in the eggs, one at a time, until incorporated. Stir in the flour mixture and yogurt alternately, in three additions, stirring until combined.

Pour the mixture into the prepared tin and bake for about 35 minutes, until a skewer inserted in the middle comes out clean. Remove from the oven and leave to cool in the tin for about 15 minutes before inverting on to a wire rack. Leave to cool completely.

To make the icing, combine all the ingredients in a bowl and stir until smooth. Spread the icing over the cooled cake, leave to set then cut into squares to serve.

TORTA AL CIOCCOLATO E NOCCIOLE

CHOCOLATE AND HAZELNUT CAKE

Nothing beats a good chocolate cake, and this one has everything that I love in a cake: it's fudgy and full of flavour, yet not too sweet. I include Frangelico liqueur in this recipe, as I do for the Roasted Cocoa Cake on page 186, which is a hazelnut liqueur from Piedmont dating back 300 years. The story goes that monks living in the area were great connoisseurs of the wild hazelnuts found in the region, and made good use of them in various preparations. Once you've made this, you will definitely make it again, and again, and again!

Note: If you make the ganache in advance and refrigerate it, you will need to soften it before applying it to the cake. Reheat it in a saucepan over a very gentle heat until softened.

Serves 10–12

Ingredients

A little softened butter, for greasing

Edible gold leaf, to decorate (optional)

For the ganache and filling

500ml *(2 scant cups)* double *(heavy)* cream

500g *(1lb 2oz)* dark chocolate, finely chopped

300g *(11oz)* ground hazelnuts

For the cake

400g *(3⅓ cups)* plain *(all-purpose)* flour, sifted

400g *(2 cups)* caster *(granulated)* sugar

1¼ tablespoons bicarbonate of soda *(baking soda)*

½ teaspoon salt

125g *(1¼ cups)* good-quality cocoa powder

300ml *(1¼ cups)* vegetable oil

300ml *(1¼ cups)* buttermilk

1 teaspoon vanilla paste or extract

3 eggs

For the chocolate glaze

160ml *(⅔ cup)* light corn syrup (or golden syrup)

2 tablespoons Frangelico liqueur

2 tablespoons water

300g *(10oz)* dark chocolate, finely chopped

Method

Prepare the ganache. Place the cream in a pan over a medium heat and bring to a boil. Remove and add the chopped chocolate. Using a balloon whisk, gently stir until melted and smooth. Cover the bowl with cling film (plastic wrap) and leave to cool to a spreadable consistency, about 2 hours.

Preheat the oven to 180°C/350°F. Butter the insides of two 20-cm/8-inch cake tins and line the bases with baking parchment.

Place the flour, sugar, bicarbonate of soda, salt and cocoa powder in the bowl of a stand mixer fitted with a paddle attachment. On a low speed, mix until blended. In a jug, put the oil, buttermilk, vanilla and eggs and whisk until blended. Turn the mixer back on and add the liquid ingredients to the dry to mix. Divide between the tins and bake for 35 minutes, until a skewer inserted into the middle comes out with a few wet crumbs attached. Leave to cool in the tins.

To assemble, place one cooled cake on a plate. Spread a layer of ganache on top and sprinkle the ground hazelnuts over the surface. Place the second cake on top. Using a spatula, spread the remaining ganache over the top and sides of the cake to create an even coating. Use a cake side scraper to smooth the sides and edges. Refrigerate to set.

For the chocolate glaze, whisk the corn syrup with the Frangelico and water in a saucepan and bring to a boil. Put the chopped chocolate in a large heatproof bowl and pour over the hot syrup. Stir to melt and mix.

Remove the cake from the fridge. Pour the glaze onto the centre of the cake, allowing it to coat the top and drip down the sides. Spread to coat evenly, using a spatula. Repeat the action until the top and sides are perfectly smooth. Allow to set, then decorate with edible gold leaf, if you wish.

TORTA MIELE E LIQUORE PERSICHETTO

HONEY AND PERSICHETTO LIQUEUR CAKE

There is a place not far from where I live that belongs to dear friends and amazing wine makers. It is called Ca'Lunae, an internationally acclaimed winery where they also produce all sorts of amazing food, such as olive oil, jams, artisan cookies, and much more besides. I am a big fan of their Persichetto, a sweet liqueur made with peach tree leaves. It has such a delicate aroma, perfect as an after-dinner digestif or as an aperitif.

Summer at Ca'Lunae means wine tasting... A lot of wine tasting, with picnics on the grass eating local organic products and chatting with friends. Quintessential Italian lifestyle! So, this cake is for D and D. Thank you for what you do and thank you for being such nice people!

Note: You can find Persichetto in good wine shops or online from Ca'Lunae at www.cantinelunae.it.

Serves 10–12

Ingredients

For the Persichetto syrup
200g (*1 cup*) caster (*granulated*) sugar

200ml (*¾ cup plus 1 tablespoon*) water

2 tablespoons Persichetto liqueur

For the cake
Melted butter, for greasing

400g (*3 cups*) plain (*all-purpose*) flour, sifted, plus extra for dusting

2 teaspoons baking powder

½ teaspoon salt

250g (*1 cup plus 2 tablespoons*) butter, at room temperature

200g (*1 cup*) caster (*granulated*) sugar

240g (*1 cup*) sour cream

1 teaspoon vanilla paste or extract

60ml (*¼ cup*) clear honey, such as acacia

Finely grated zest of 1 orange

4 eggs

245ml (*1 cup*) milk

120ml (*½ cup*) Persichetto liqueur

Toasted flaked (*slivered*) almonds, to decorate (optional)

Method

Preheat the oven to 180°C/350°F. Brush melted butter liberally over the insides of a large bundt cake tin, the design/shape of your choice, making sure you get into every crevice. Then sprinkle flour inside the tin, tilting and rotating it to distribute it evenly.

For the syrup, put the sugar and water into a medium saucepan set over a medium heat and heat until the sugar has completely dissolved. Cook for a further minute then take off the heat and add the Persichetto. Allow to cool while you make the cake.

Sift the flour, baking powder and salt into a mixing bowl and set side. In the bowl of a stand mixer, or using another mixing bowl and electric hand-held beaters, beat together the butter, sugar, sour cream, vanilla, honey and orange zest until combined. Beat in the eggs one at a time.

Add the flour mixture and, with the beaters running on a slow speed, add the milk and Persichetto. Pour the batter into the prepared tin and bake for about 40–45 minutes, until a skewer inserted in the middle comes out clean. Leave to cool in the tin before inverting on to a serving plate. Brush the cake generously with the Persichetto syrup and sprinkle the toasted almonds over the cake to serve.

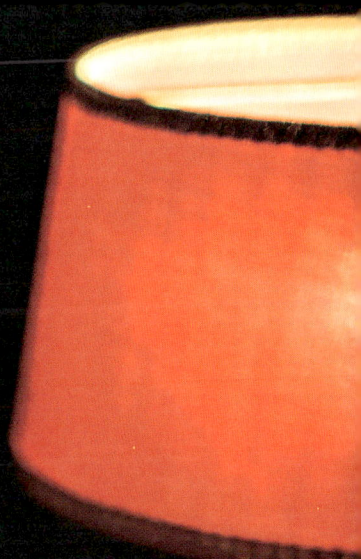

BROWNIES AL RISO VENERE

BROWNIES WITH BLACK VENERE RICE

I came up with the idea of adding black Venere rice while thinking about two of my favourite ingredients: chocolate and rice. Riso Venere is a type of black rice created in Italy in 1997 from a hybrid of Chinese Black rice and a variety from the Pianura Padana region in the north of Italy. The result is a nutty tasting, bread-scented rice, available in delicatessen shops all over the world. These decadent and exotic brownies are fudgy but still retain a cakey texture. And did I mention that black Venere rice is a good source of fibre? Cool, huh?

Makes 16

Ingredients

350g *(1½ cups)* unsalted butter, at room temperature, plus extra for greasing

180g *(6oz)* black Venere rice

150g *(5oz)* good-quality dark chocolate, cut into small chunks

450g *(2¼ cups)* caster *(granulated)* sugar

200g *(2 cups)* good-quality cocoa powder

6 eggs

200g *(1½ cups plus 2 tablespoons)* plain *(all-purpose)* flour, sifted

A pinch of salt

Method

Preheat the oven to 180°C/350°F. Butter the base and sides of a 30-cm/12-inch square cake tin or two 15-cm/6-inch tins, 8cm/3 inches deep.

Rinse the rice under cold water then place it in a pan with double its volume of water and cook for 40 minutes or until the rice is actually overcooked (so that it won't turn crisp during baking).

Put the chocolate in a heatproof bowl and melt either in a microwave or over a pan of simmering water (making sure the bowl isn't touching the water). Stir, then set aside and leave to cool at room temperature.

In a bowl of a stand mixer, or using electric hand-held beaters and a mixing bowl, beat the butter and sugar together until pale and fluffy. Add the cocoa powder and beat on a slow speed until it is incorporated.

Beat in the eggs, one at a time, then add the cooled melted chocolate and beat. Now add the flour and salt and beat only until it is incorporated; do not overwork the mixture. Finally, stir in the cooked rice using a large spoon or spatula. Pour the batter into the tin/s and bake for 30–35 minutes, until a skewer inserted in the middle comes out slightly smeared – the brownies need to seem slightly undercooked in order to be fudgy.

Leave to cool completely in the tin/s before cutting into squares.

TORTA AL LIMONE, LAMPONI E ROSMARINO

LEMON, RASPBERRY AND ROSEMARY CAKE

Now, this is a truly international cake! It's layered (the American way), the sponge is close to an Italian *pan di Spagna* sponge, the lemon and rosemary are truly Mediterranean, while the raspberries come from the forests of central Europe. It's fresh, light and has a balsamic scent. Wonderful for tea with friends or a birthday party, and if you serve it at the end of a meal you can be sure of a showstopper!

Serves 10–12

Ingredients

For the syrup
200g *(1 cup)* caster *(granulated)* sugar

200ml *(¾ cup)* water

125g *(4oz)* rosemary sprigs, plus extra to decorate

For the sponge
A little softened butter, for greasing

8 eggs, at room temperature

160g *(just over ¾ cup)* caster *(granulated)* sugar

1 teaspoon vanilla paste or extract

160g *(just over 1¼ cups)* plain *(all-purpose)* flour, sifted

1 teaspoon baking powder

Finely grated zest of 1 lemon

For the filling
350g *(12oz)* frozen raspberries, plus extra (fresh) to decorate

1 teaspoon cornflour *(cornstarch)*

2 tablespoons freshly squeezed lemon juice

60g *(scant ⅓ cup)* caster *(granulated)* sugar

For the frosting
250ml *(1 cup)* double *(heavy)* cream

250g *(9oz)* mascarpone cheese

90g *(¾ cup)* icing *(confectioner's)* sugar, sifted, plus extra to decorate

Method

Make the syrup. Put the sugar and water in a pan over a medium heat. Heat for 15–20 minutes until the sugar has completely dissolved. Add the rosemary, cover and leave to infuse. Once cooled to room temperature, chill in the fridge overnight.

Preheat the oven to 180°C/350°F. Butter the bases and sides of two 20-cm/8-inch cake tins and line with baking parchment.

Put the eggs, sugar and vanilla into the bowl of a stand mixer (or use a mixing bowl and electric hand-held beaters) and beat until doubled in volume, about 6 minutes. Now gradually fold in the flour by hand.

Divide the batter between the prepared tins and bake for about 25–30 minutes, until a skewer inserted in the middle comes out clean and the cakes are springy to the touch. Remove from the oven and leave to cool in the tins for 10 minutes before inverting on to a wire rack to cool completely.

Combine all the filling ingredients in a small pan and slowly bring to a boil over a medium heat, stirring constantly until it thickens. Remove from the heat and cool completely.

For the frosting, whip the cream until medium-stiff. Put the mascarpone and icing sugar in the bowl of a stand mixer (or in a mixing bowl with an electric hand-held whisk) fitted with the paddle attachment and mix for about 3 minutes on a slow-medium speed. Add the whipped cream and mix on a high speed for about 3 more minutes.

To assemble, brush syrup over each cake and let it soak in. Pipe a ring of frosting around the first layer to create a ridge, and spoon the filling into the middle. Repeat with a second layer of sponge. Frost the cake as you wish, decorate with rosemary and raspberries and dust with icing sugar.

CHEESECAKE AL PISTACCHIO E LAMPONI

PISTACHIO AND RASPBERRY CHEESECAKE

I use *Pistacchi di Bronte* here, from Bronte in Sicily. These little gems explode with flavour! You can use any pistachios you happen to find, but if you get the chance to buy the Bronte variety, grab them fast.

This cheesecake says "summer" to me, and it celebrates once again all that is dear to me: my mother-country Italy, England which has adopted me, and America where I spent two important years of my life. Enjoy!

Ingredients

For the crust

60g (*about ½ cup*) shelled pistachios

160g (*5½ oz*) digestive biscuits or Graham crackers

80g (*⅓ cup*) butter, melted

For the filling

900g (*about 4 cups*) cream cheese

270g (*2¼ cups*) icing (*confectioner's*) sugar, sifted

2 tablespoons cornflour (*cornstarch*)

½ teaspoon salt

5 eggs

250g (*1 cup*) sour cream

2 teaspoons vanilla paste or extract

250g (*1 cup*) double (*heavy*) cream

To decorate

110g (*⅓ cup*) apricot jam

150g (*1 cup*) shelled pistachios

At least 250g (*1 cup*) raspberries, depending how big they are

Method

Preheat the oven to 180°C (350°F). Butter the base and sides of a 23-cm/9-inch springform cake tin. Wrap foil tightly all around the outside of the tin to make it watertight.

For the crust, put all the ingredients in a food processor and pulse until they resemble breadcrumbs. Press the crumbs into the bottom of the prepared tin and bake for 10–15 minutes. Remove from the oven and leave to cool completely. Leave the oven on.

For the filling, beat the cream cheese in the bowl of a stand mixer until smooth. In a separate bowl, sift together the icing sugar, cornstarch and salt, then gradually beat into the cream cheese. Add the eggs, one at the time, on low speed. Finally, beat in the sour cream, vanilla and double cream.

Pour the mixture into the tin over the baked crust. Place the tin inside a larger one and fill the larger one with hot water to come about halfway up the cheesecake tin. This is a water bath and it helps to bake the cheesecake gently and evenly. Bake for 60 minutes until the top feels firm.

Remove the tin from its water bath and peel away the foil. Leave the cheesecake to cool completely in the tin on a wire rack, then transfer to the fridge and chill for at least 4 hours, or overnight. Once chilled, run a knife around the edge of the cheesecake and release it from the tin on to a plate.

When you are ready to serve, heat the jam until runny, then strain through a sieve. Brush the jam all over the cake. In a food processor, roughly chop the pistachios. Holding the cake up with one hand, press the chopped pistachios all around the side of the cake. Cover the top with raspberries.

TORTA AL FORMAGGIO SPECIALE

SPECIAL CREAM-CHEESE POUND CAKE

Who says complicated things are the best? I strongly believe the opposite. But while I think simple is better, it can be mistaken for easy, which is not always the case. Simple ingredients, simple technique, simple decoration. These are the things this cake is made of. I found this recipe in an old cooking magazine and since discovering it can't live without it!

Serves 8–10

Ingredients

340g (*1½ cups*) butter, softened, plus extra for greasing

420g (*3 cups*) plain (*all-purpose*) flour, plus extra for dusting

225g (*8oz*) cream cheese

500g (*2½ cups*) caster (*superfine*) sugar

Grated zest of 1 lemon

6 eggs

2 teaspoons vanilla paste or extract

Method

Preheat the oven to 160°C/320°F.

Using a pastry brush, butter a bundt tin, making sure you get into every crevice. Dust with flour then tilt and rotate the tin to completely and evenly coat the insides. Tip out any excess of flour.

In the bowl of a stand mixer, or in a mixing bowl and using electric hand-held beaters, beat the butter and cream cheese together until creamy. Add the sugar and beat on a high speed until fluffy. Add the lemon zest, reduce the mixer speed and add the eggs and flour alternately in three additions.

Stir in the vanilla and transfer the mixture to the prepared tin. Bake for 1½ hours, checking for doneness after 1 hour. It's done when a skewer inserted in the cake comes out clean.

BUNDT CAKE AL MARSALA E PRUGNE

MARSALA PRUNE CAKE

The story goes that an English trader named John Woodhouse docked his ship in 1773 in the Sicilian port of Marsala, where the locals were making a sweet wine named after the town. He liked it so much he decided to load the ship with 50 barrels to bring back to England. He also decided to fortify the wine with a type of grappa, to make it stronger and so it would last the ocean voyage. The English loved it very much and so Woodhouse returned to Sicily and started trading for the British market. This cake is simple and yet full of wonderful aromas. Perfect for 5 o'clock tea.

Serves 8–10

Ingredients

130g (*½ cup*) butter, at room temperature, plus extra for greasing

250g (*9oz*) prunes, chopped and stones removed

125ml (*½ cup*) Marsala

230g (*1 cup plus 2 tablespoons*) light brown sugar

2 eggs

150g (*5½oz*) sour cream

230g (*1¾ cups plus 1 tablespoon*) plain (*all-purpose*) flour

3 teaspoons baking powder

Method

Preheat the oven to 160°C/320°F. Butter a 20-cm/8-inch bundt tin, making sure it goes into every crevice.

Put the chopped prunes and Marsala in a saucepan set over a medium heat and cook for about 20 minutes. Remove and set aside to cool a little before processing to a smooth purée in a food processor or blender.

Meanwhile, in the bowl of a stand mixer, or in a mixing bowl and using hand-held electric beaters, beat the butter and sugar together until light and fluffy. Beat in the eggs one at a time. Add the sour cream and beat until combined. Sift the flour, add the baking powder and gradually beat into the wet mixture; do not over-beat. Stir the prune purée into the mixture until combined.

Transfer the mixture to the prepared tin, smooth the surface using a spatula and bake for 50 minutes until a skewer inserted in the cake comes out clean. Once baked, leave to cool in the tin for about 10 minutes before inverting on to a wire rack to cool completely.

BISCOTTI AL COCCO FACILI

EASY COCONUT COOKIES

This recipe comes from my Aunt Rose's cookbook. She is from the Philippines and used to make masses of these cookies back when she lived there. She was kind enough to give me this recipe when I was a young girl and wanted to bake but didn't have the confidence that I have now. It's a foolproof recipe and fun to make with your kids.

Makes about 40

Ingredients

3 egg whites

150g (¾ *cup*) caster (*superfine*) sugar

250g (*9oz*) finely shredded desiccated coconut

A pinch of salt

Method

Preheat the oven to 170°C/335°F. Line a large baking sheet with baking parchment. Fit a piping bag with a plain nozzle. I use a Wilton 1A or Ateco 806 large round tip.

In the bowl of a stand mixer fitted with a whisk attachment (or using a mixing bowl and hand-held electric whisk), whisk the egg whites until frothy. Add the sugar and whisk until stiff peaks form. Fold in the desiccated coconut.

Fill the prepared piping bag with the mixture and pipe rounds directly on the baking parchment, leaving some space between each cookie.

Bake for about 15 minutes until golden. Leave to cool completely on the baking sheet (if you touch them when still warm they will break). Delicious dropped into yogurt, or served on a mountain of ice cream!

BUNDT CAKE AL CIOCCOLATO RIPIENA DI FORMAGGIO

CREAM CHEESE-FILLED CHOCOLATE BUNDT CAKE

My customers at the shop love everything I bake with cream cheese. There is something about cream-cheese cakes that is hard to explain – maybe it's the tangy flavour paired with deep, dark chocolate, or just the creaminess the cheese provides. The fact is, any cake made with cream cheese has something extra, and this bundt cake is no exception. Not only are bundt cakes designed to be a stunning centrepiece on the table, but they are also fun to make.

Serves 10–12

Ingredients

For the filling

250g *(9oz)* cream cheese

135g *(²/₃ cup)* caster (*granulated*) sugar

1 egg

1 teaspoon vanilla paste or extract

2 teaspoons plain (*all-purpose*) flour

For the cake

140g *(5oz)* good-quality dark chocolate, finely chopped

80g *(¾ cup)* good-quality cocoa powder, plus extra for dusting

180ml *(¾ cup)* boiling water

280g *(2 cups)* plain (*all-purpose*) flour, sifted

1 teaspoon salt

1 teaspoon bicarbonate of soda (*baking soda*)

250g *(1 cup)* sour cream

170g *(¾ cup)* butter, at room temperature, plus extra for greasing

400g *(2 cups)* caster (*granulated*) sugar

1 teaspoon vanilla paste or extract

5 eggs, at room temperature

For the glaze

120ml *(½ cup)* double (*heavy*) cream

2 teaspoons golden syrup

110g *(4oz)* good-quality dark chocolate, finely chopped

Method

Preheat the oven to 180°C/350°F. Butter a large bundt tin with softened butter and dust with cocoa powder, tilting the tin and rotating it to make sure it is fully coated, then tipping out any excess cocoa powder.

For the filling, put the cream cheese and sugar in the bowl of a stand mixer (or use a mixing bowl and electric hand-held beaters) and beat until combined. Add the egg, vanilla and flour and beat to combine. Set aside.

For the cake, combine the cocoa powder and chopped chocolate in a heatproof bowl. Pour over the boiling water and gently stir until the chocolate is fully melted. Set aside to cool.

In another bowl, mix together the flour, salt and bicarbonate of soda. Now stir the sour cream into the cooled chocolate mixture and set aside.

In the bowl of stand mixer fitted with a paddle attachment, beat the butter, sugar and vanilla together until fluffy, then beat in the eggs, one a time. Stir in the flour mixture followed by the chocolate mixture, until mixture is smooth.

Pour a little of the mixture into the prepared bundt tin. Spread cream cheese filling over the cake mixture, making sure you don't pipe as far as the edges, or it will leak out during baking.

Pour the remaining cake mixture over the filling and bake for 45 minutes until a skewer inserted in the cake comes out clean. Remove from the oven and leave to cool completely in the tin.

To make the glaze, put the cream and syrup in a saucepan and bring to a boil, then add the chocolate and stir to combine. Drizzle over the cooled cake and leave to set.

LA MIA TORTA DI NATALE AMERICANA

MY AMERICAN CHRISTMAS CAKE

Every Christmas, while I cook for my family and friends, I wonder how many people are doing the same, and I feel we are all connected through a single purpose: showing our love through cooking. In Italy, Christmas is a big deal and the table is literally overloaded with food. We do have amazing recipes for Christmas cakes, but this cake can be easily added to the menu without sacrificing any other dessert. It is tradition here to have meals of at least four courses and many desserts.

In this cake I use an Italian eggy liqueur called VOV, which is basically a mixture of Marsala and eggs and can be considered the Italian version of eggnog. A note: the base recipe for this sponge cake is the same as for the Lemon and Mascarpone cake on page 206; the recipe is so versatile you can add new ingredients every time.

Serves 12–14

Ingredients

For the cakes

A little softened butter, for greasing

285g (*2 cups plus 2 tablespoons*) plain (*all-purpose*) flour

1½ teaspoons baking powder

200g (*1 cup*) caster (*granulated*) sugar

4 eggs, separated

¼ teaspoon cream of tartar

A pinch of salt

100ml (*scant ½ cup*) vegetable oil

100ml (*scant ½ cup*) water, at room temperature

Grated zest of 1 large orange

1 teaspoon ground cinnamon

1 teaspoon ground nutmeg

1 teaspoon vanilla paste or extract

For the frosting and filling

250ml (*generous 1 cup*) double (*heavy*) cream

250g (*9oz*) mascarpone cheese

3–4 tablespoons VOV liqueur or eggnog, to taste

90g (*¾ cup*) icing (*confectioner's*) sugar

Method

Preheat the oven to 180°C/350°F. Butter two 20-cm/8-inch cake tins and line the bases and sides with baking parchment.

Sift the flour into a medium bowl, add the baking powder and half the sugar and whisk to combine. Set aside. Place the egg whites in a large bowl, add the cream of tartar and set aside.

Put the yolks in the bowl of a stand mixer fitted with a paddle attachment. Add the salt, oil, water, orange zest, cinnamon, nutmeg and vanilla and beat until mixed. Add the flour mixture and beat for 1 minute or until well mixed (do not over-mix).

Using an electric hand-held whisk, whisk the egg whites until frothy, then add the remaining sugar and whisk until stiff peaks form. Fold the whisked egg whites very gently into the cake batter, then divide the mixture between the prepared tins and bake in the oven for 20–25 minutes until a skewer inserted into the middle comes out clean. Leave to cool in the tins for 10 minutes before turning out on to a wire rack to cool completely.

For the frosting and filling, whip the cream until medium-stiff. Put the mascarpone and liqueur (I like all 4 tablespoons!) in a separate bowl and beat until creamy. Add the icing sugar and beat until incorporated. Finally, add the whipped cream to the mascarpone mixture and beat just enough so the ingredients are well blended; do not over-beat. If it's too runny, add more icing sugar.

To assemble, place one cake on a plate. Spread over some filling and top with the second cake. Cover the entire cake with mascarpone cream, using a spatula and decorating with a piped edge if you like (and a sugarpaste stag painted with edible gold dust!)

BISCOTTI SENZA UOVA

EGG-FREE COOKIES

A few of my regular customers down at the bakery are egg intolerant, so I came up with this recipe for them to be able to enjoy a good cup of tea and a cookie in our tea room. Use this recipe as a base for countless variations.

Makes 12–15

Ingredients

200g (1½ cups plus 2 tablespoons) plain (all-purpose) flour, sifted, plus extra for dusting

50g (¼ cup) caster (granulated) sugar

100g (⅓ cup plus 1½ tablespoons) butter, melted

1 teaspoon vanilla paste or extract

Finely grated zest of 2 lemons or 1 teaspoon pure lemon extract

1 teaspoon baking powder

60ml (¼ cup) milk

Method

Preheat the oven to 160°C/320°F. Line a baking sheet with baking parchment.

In a large bowl, combine all the ingredients and form them into a dough using your hands. As soon as the dough comes together, stop kneading. On a lightly floured surface, roll the dough out to about 1cm/½ inch thick and stamp out rounds using a medium-sized round or square cutter.

Place the cut out cookies on the lined baking sheet and bake for about 6–10 minutes until golden, longer if you prefer them more crunchy, or less if you like them pale and soft. Leave to cool on the baking sheet before removing.

TORTA DI FIORI DI VIOLETTE

VIOLET FLOWER CAKE

I'm simply in love with edible flowers, and have been using them recently in cakes, puddings and cookies; I encourage you to do the same. They are pure magic, pure beauty and pure taste. My friend L is a so-called "nose", someone who studies and makes perfumes using only the best ingredients and lots of flowers and spices. I love her bespoke fragrances and she loves my cakes. This cake is dedicated to her, for always surrounding me with wonderful floral aromas.

Serves 12–14

Ingredients

For the vanilla syrup

120ml (½ cup) water

120g (½ cup plus 2 tablespoons) caster (granulated) sugar

1 teaspoon vanilla paste or the seeds of 1 vanilla pod

For the sponge cake

A little softened butter, for greasing

120g (scant 1 cup) plain (all-purpose) flour

4 eggs

A pinch of salt

120g (½ cup plus 2 tablespoons) caster (granulated) sugar

1 teaspoon vanilla paste or extract

Grated zest of 1 lemon

For the filling and topping

250g (9oz) fresh mixed fruits of the forest, plus extra to decorate

2 tablespoons lemon juice

1 tablespoon caster (granulated) sugar

500ml (generous 2 cups) double (heavy) cream

A generous handful of edible violets, plus extra to decorate

Method

To prepare the vanilla syrup, put the water and sugar into a pan and set over a medium heat until the sugar is fully dissolved. Increase the heat and, as soon as it comes to a boil, remove from the heat, add the vanilla and set aside to cool.

Preheat the oven to 180°C/350°F. Butter two 20-cm/8-inch cake tins and line the bases with baking parchment. Sift the flour three times.

In the bowl of a stand mixer, or in a mixing bowl and using hand-held electric beaters, beat the eggs, salt and sugar until quadrupled in volume. This will take 15–20 minutes but is a crucial step, so be patient. Beat in the vanilla and lemon zest.

Very gently fold in the sifted flower in small additions, using a spatula and trying not to deflate the mixture. Once fully incorporated, divide the mixture between the prepared tins and bake for 25–30 minutes until a skewer inserted in the middle of the cakes comes out clean. Remove from the oven and leave to cool for 10 minutes in the tins before inverting on to a wire rack.

Put the fruits of the forest into a bowl, add the lemon juice and sugar and gently stir to avoid breaking them up. In a separate bowl, whip the cream for the frosting to a stiff consistency.

To assemble, place one of the cakes on a plate. Prick the entire surface with a skewer and brush with a generous amount of vanilla syrup. Spread over an even layer of whipped cream, place the fruits in the centre and push them just a little towards the sides (not too near the edge or they will leak out when you stack the cake). Top with violets and stack the other cake on top. Spread the remaining whipped cream over the top and sides of the cake. Decorate with extra violets and some more fruits.

CROSTATA DI MELISSA

MELISSA'S TART

This is a summery alternative to a lemon tart, perfect for a picnic or for tea in the garden. The lemon balm adds a sophisticated aroma as well as bringing other benefits to the mind and body. In Italian, it is called *melissa*, so it was just natural for me to try baking with it. Such a pleasant discovery!

Serves 8–10

Ingredients

For the pastry

300g *(scant 2½ cups)* plain *(all-purpose)* flour

150g *(⅔ cup)* butter, chilled and diced, plus a little extra, softened, for greasing

120g *(½ cup plus 1 tablespoon)* caster *(granulated)* sugar

2 whole eggs plus 1 yolk

A pinch of salt

Grated zest of 1 lemon

For the lemon balm custard filling

250ml *(generous 1 cup)* double *(heavy)* cream

250ml *(generous 1 cup)* milk

20–30g *(about 1oz)* fresh lemon balm leaves

Grated zest of 1 lemon

8 egg yolks

100g *(½ cup)* caster *(granulated)* sugar

Method

Heap the flour in a mound on the work surface and make a well in the centre. Add the diced butter to the well and rub it into the flour using your fingertips until it reaches a crumble consistency. Make a well in the middle again and add the sugar, eggs plus yolk, salt and lemon zest. Work the dough as briefly as possible until all the ingredients are incorporated and form a dough. Wrap in cling film (plastic wrap) and refrigerate for at least 1 hour, or better still overnight.

Butter a 20-cm/8-inch tart tin with a removable base. Roll out the chilled pastry into a circle about 2.5cm/1 inch thick. Place it over the tart tin and press the sides and base gently into the tin. Trim off any excess pastry. Prick the base in a few places with a fork and chill the pastry case in the fridge.

Meanwhile, prepare the custard. Put the cream, milk, lemon balm leaves and lemon zest in a saucepan set over medium heat and bring to a boil. Take off the heat, cover with a lid and leave to infuse for 10 minutes.

Preheat the oven to 160°C/320°F. Beat the egg yolks and sugar together until pale, in the bowl of a stand mixer or in a mixing bowl and using electric hand-held beaters, then pour in the warm milky mixture and continue to beat on a slow speed until blended. Strain the custard through a fine sieve and discard the leaves. Set aside.

Line the pastry case with foil or baking parchment and fill with ceramic or dried beans. Bake in the oven for 10 minutes, then take out of the oven and remove the foil or paper and the beans. Bake the pastry case for a further 10 minutes, then pour in the custard and bake for 20 minutes or until set.

Leave the tart to cool in the tin before removing to a plate to serve, at room temperature or cold.

FETTA DI MARMELLATA DI MORE CON MANDORLE

BLACKBERRY AND ALMOND SLICES

My father used to take me blackberry picking in the woods when I was small. We would return home with baskets full of berries, as well as grazes from the thorny bushes. We would then make *marmellata di more*, or blackberry jam, to turn into a blackberry tart – one of my favourite things in the world! This variation on the classic tart brings back so many sweet memories...

Makes 12 slices or 6 large squares

Ingredients

100g (*⅓ cup plus 1½ tablespoons*) butter, plus extra for greasing

100g (*½ cup*) caster (*granulated*) sugar

1 teaspoon vanilla paste or extract

Finely grated zest of 1 lemon

160g (*1⅓ cups*) plain (*all-purpose*) flour

1 teaspoon baking powder

350g (*1 cup*) good-quality blackberry jam, ideally homemade

1 egg

75g (*3oz*) ground almonds

250g (*9oz*) flaked (*slivered*) almonds

Icing (*confectioner's*) sugar, for dusting (optional)

Method

Preheat the oven to 160°C/320°F. Butter the base and sides of a 20 x 30-cm/8 x 12-inch baking tin. Line with a large piece of baking parchment, allowing it to hang over the sides by about 5cm/ 2 inches all round.

In the bowl of a stand mixer, or in a mixing bowl using a hand-held electric beaters, beat the butter, sugar, vanilla and lemon zest together until pale and fluffy.

Sift the flour and baking powder into a separate bowl, then beat it, little by little, into the mixture. Transfer the mixture to the lined tin and spread it out evenly, using a spatula. Still using a spatula, spread the jam over the surface of the base, going right to the edges.

Crack the egg into a clean bowl and whisk slightly with a fork. Add the ground almonds and just a small amount of the flaked almonds, reserving the majority for the top, and stir to mix. Spread the mixture over the jam in an even layer. Finally, sprinkle the remaining flaked almonds evenly over the top and bake in the oven for 35–40 minutes, until the flaked almonds are a deep golden colour and the base is cooked through.

Remove from the oven and leave to cool in the tin, then use the overhanging parchment to lift it out of tin and cut into slices or squares. Sprinkle with icing sugar if you like.

TORTA PESCHE E AMARETTO

NECTARINE AND AMARETTO CAKE

Very few things say summer to me more than nectarines. In Italy we produce some very fine ones... so juicy and sweet! Amaretto loves nectarines, and I hope you will love this cake.

Serves 8

Ingredients

200g (*scant 1 cup*) butter, at room temperature, plus extra for greasing

2–3 nectarines, depending on size

200g (*1 cup*) caster (*granulated*) sugar

50g (*¼ cup*) light brown sugar

1 teaspoon vanilla paste or extract

Finely grated zest of 1 lemon

2 eggs

1½ tablespoons Amaretto or other almond liqueur, plus extra to finish (latter optional)

200g (*1½ cups plus 2 tablespoons*) plain (*all-purpose*) flour

50g (*⅓ cup*) ground almonds

1½ teaspoons baking powder

100ml (*⅓ cup plus 1½ tablespoons*) milk

300g (*11oz*) chopped almonds

Icing (*confectioner's*) sugar, for dusting

Method

Preheat the oven to 160°C/320°F. Butter a 20-cm/8-inch cake tin and line with baking parchment.

Cut the nectarines in half, remove the stones and cut the nectarines in thin slices. Put into a bowl and set aside.

In the bowl of stand mixer, or using a mixing bowl and hand-held electric beaters, cream the butter and both sugars together until pale and fluffy. Add the vanilla and lemon zest. Beat in the eggs one at a time and continue to beat until fully incorporated. Stir in the Amaretto.

Sift the flour, ground almonds and baking powder together then fold into the mixture in three additions, alternating with the milk. Gently stir in 50g (2oz) of the chopped almonds. Transfer the mixture to the prepared tin and fan the nectarine slices out over the batter in a sunburst pattern.

Sprinkle the remaining chopped almonds all over the cake and bake for 40–45 minutes until dark golden, and caramelized in places. Leave to cool completely in the tin before inverting on to a plate. Dust with icing sugar or sprinkle with a splash of Amaretto, if you wish.

TORTA DI PANE AL CIOCCOLATO E NOCCIOLE

BREAD, CHOCOLATE AND HAZELNUT CAKE

How to make a delicious cake using leftover bread? Follow this recipe. I don't like to waste food and so, whenever I have some bread left over, I bake this cake – stale bread works perfectly in many desserts. In England bread-and-butter pudding is a solid tradition and this makes me think that; after all, we are not so different from one another. Old recipes dating from tougher times, using whatever the pantry had to offer, are a feature common to all cultures. Chocolate was once a very expensive and rare ingredient, and so originally this cake was rich in spices and nuts. This version is more contemporary, and definitely a recipe to have to hand and to pass on.

Serves 6

Ingredients

A little softened butter,
  for greasing

225g *(8oz)* stale bread, plus a
  handful of breadcrumbs

500ml *(generous 2 cups)* milk

35g *(⅓ cup)* good-quality
  cocoa powder, plus extra
  for dusting

140g *(4½oz)* ground hazelnuts

2 eggs

140g *(⅔ cup)* light muscovado
  sugar

Grated zest of 1 orange

2 tablespoons dark rum

A pinch of salt

Method

Preheat the oven to 180°C/350°F. Butter an 18-cm/7-inch, deep cake tin, sprinkle the breadcrumbs over the base and set aside.

Cut the stale bread into chunks and put into a heatproof bowl. Bring the milk to a boil in a pan, pour over the bread and leave to soak and cool. Once cooled, squeeze out any excess milk from the bread and, using a fork, break the chunks down until mashed. Set aside.

While the bread is soaking, process the cocoa powder and ground hazelnuts in a blender. Put the eggs, sugar and orange zest into a bowl and add the rum and salt. Using a balloon whisk, gently whisk the ingredients together. Using a large spoon or spatula, stir in the mashed bread and the cocoa and hazelnut mixture.

Pour the mixture into the prepared tin and bake for 40 minutes, until a skewer inserted in the middle comes out clean. Once cooled, dust generously with cocoa powder and serve.

TORTA DI RICOTTA ARANCIA E CIOCCOLATO

RICOTTA, ORANGE AND CHOCOLATE CAKE

I love ricotta cheese, especially in cakes. I also believe orange zest and chocolate are made for each other. Period.

Serves 8

Ingredients

For the ricotta filling

500g (*1lb 2oz*) ricotta cheese

250g (*1¼ cups*) caster (*granulated*) sugar

Finely grated zest of 1 orange

225g (*8oz*) chocolate chips or chopped chocolate

For the cake

200g (*scant 1 cup*) butter, plus extra, softened, for greasing

300g (*scant 2½ cups*) plain (*all-purpose*) flour

95g (*¾ cup*) cornflour (*cornstarch*)

1½ teaspoons baking powder

200g (*1 cup*) caster (*granulated*) sugar

250ml (*1 cup*) double (*heavy*) cream

2 eggs

Icing (*confectioner's*) sugar or good-quality cocoa powder, for dusting

Method

Preheat the oven to 180°C/350°F. Butter a 23-cm/9-inch cake tin and line with baking parchment.

For the filling, place a fine-mesh sieve over a bowl and press the ricotta through using the back of a spoon. Add the sugar, orange zest and chocolate chips to the bowl. Stir and set aside. Sift the flour, cornflour and baking powder into a separate bowl and set aside.

Put the butter, sugar and half the cream into another bowl and heat in the microwave until the butter has melted and the sugar dissolved. Stir, then add the remaining cream and set aside to cool for a few minutes.

Meanwhile, whisk the eggs in the bowl of a stand mixer, or in a mixing bowl and using a hand-held electric whisk, until pale and creamy. Fold in (or beat in on a low speed with the stand mixer) the sifted flour mixture in three batches, alternating with the butter and cream mixture, until fully incorporated. Transfer half of the mixture to the prepared tin and, using a spatula, spread it out evenly.

Fill a piping bag with the ricotta mixture and pipe it across the centre of the cake mixture in the tin. Spread it out a little using a spatula, but try not to reach the sides of the tin. Add the remaining cake mixture on top of the ricotta mixture and spread it out evenly.

Bake in the oven for about 45 minutes until a skewer inserted in the middle comes out clean. Leave to cool completely in the tin before inverting on to a plate. Dust with either icing sugar or cocoa powder, depending on preference.

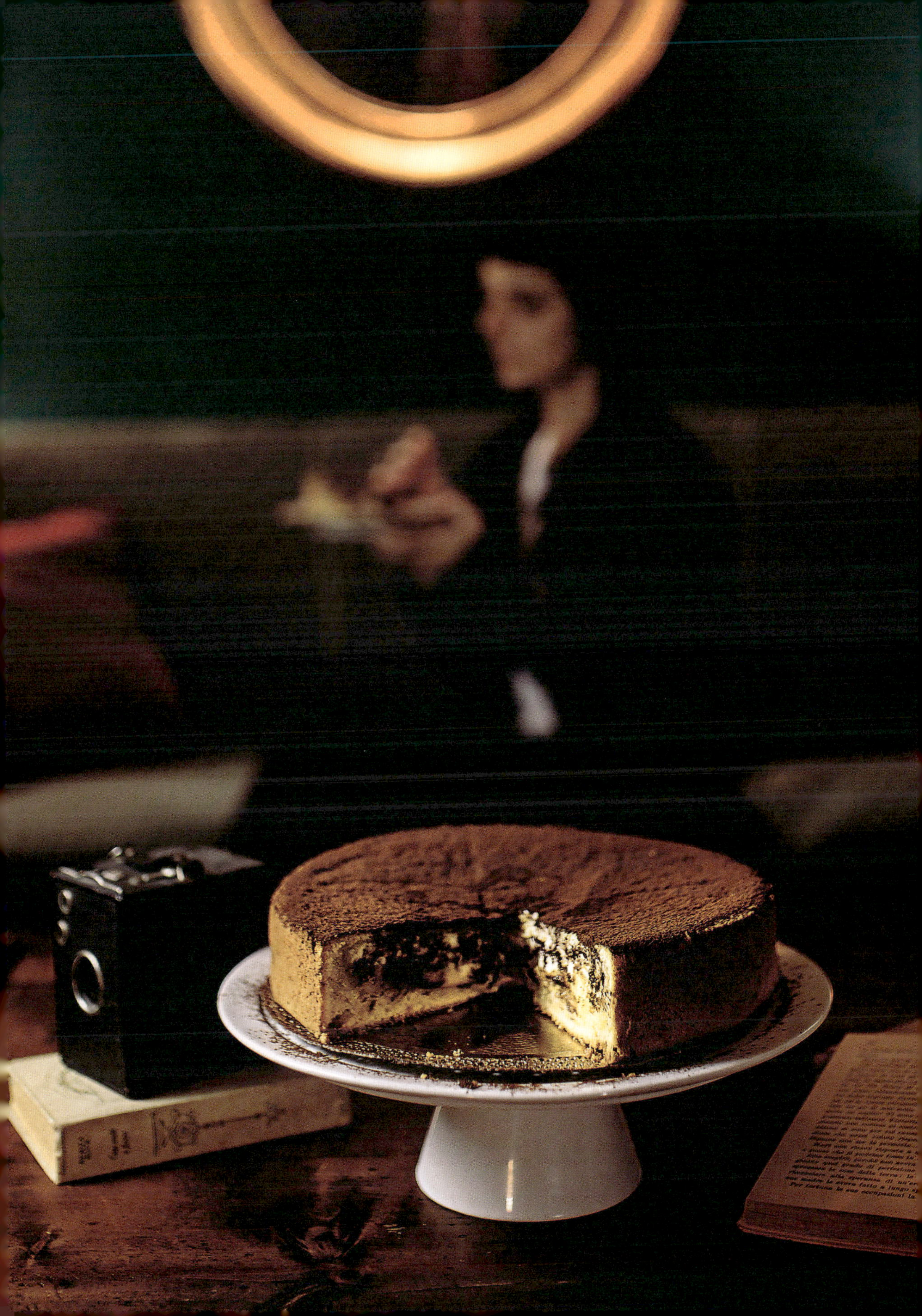

TORTA ALLO ZENZERO E SCIROPPO AL LIMONE

GINGER CAKE WITH LEMON SYRUP

A lot of my baking is about lemons. I use them in everything and I do not intend to stop! I always keep some zest and juice in the freezer for when I can't get organic lemons out of season, and often use ginger as a substitute. A good ginger and lemon loaf on a winter's afternoon is ideal for thinking about the sun…

Serves 8–10

Ingredients

200g *(scant 1 cup)* butter, at room temperature, plus extra for greasing

250g *(2 cups)* plain *(all-purpose)* flour, plus extra for dusting

200g *(1 cup)* caster *(granulated)* sugar

Finely grated zest and juice of 2 lemons

About 25g *(1oz)* freshly grated ginger

1 teaspoon vanilla paste or extract

3 eggs

2 teaspoons baking powder

4 tablespoons icing *(confectioner's)* sugar

Method

Preheat the oven to 170°C/335°F. Butter the base and sides of a 1lb loaf tin, or any other tin shape you like (I use a milk loaf tin) and dust with flour.

In the bowl of a stand mixer, or using a mixing bowl and electric hand-held beaters, beat the butter, sugar, lemon zest, ginger and vanilla together until light and fluffy. Beat in the eggs, one at a time.

Sift the flour into a bowl and add the baking powder, then fold in (or beat in on a low speed with the stand mixer) the sifted flour in three batches. Transfer to the prepared tin and bake for 40–45 minutes, until golden and a skewer inserted in the middle comes out clean. Turn the cake out onto a wire rack to cool.

Meanwhile, make the glaze. Put the icing sugar into a small pan over a low heat and gradually add the lemon juice to make a very runny, but tangy, syrup. Once the icing sugar has dissolved, take the pan off the heat. Prick the loaf all over using a skewer and slowly pour the glaze onto the loaf, allowing it to penetrate into the holes and moisten the cake.

Leave to cool completely, then serve with some whipped cream, custard or fresh fruit.

TORTA SPEZIATA DELLE FESTE

SPICED FESTIVE CAKE

Christmas is very important to me. Over the festive period, the kitchen at the bakery works constantly, as does the one in my home! They are busy days, and I love hosting parties with friends, chatting in front of the fire sipping mulled wine, organizing the table and decorating the tree.

Baking is an essential part of the celebrations, and here is a recipe for a delicious end to a generous meal – a cake that will look stunning as the table centrepiece but that is still quick to prepare. You can bake it a day in advance and reheat it by heating the oven on medium-high for 20 minutes, switching it off and putting the cake in for 5–10 minutes. Serve with custard or zabaione cream. Merry Christmas!

Serves 8–10

Ingredients

200g *(scant 1 cup)* butter, at room temperature, plus extra for greasing

250g *(2 cups)* plain *(all-purpose)* flour, plus extra for dusting

2 teaspoons baking powder

200g *(1 cup)* caster *(granulated)* sugar

2½ tablespoons ground cinnamon

2 cloves, crushed

1 teaspoon ground nutmeg

Finely grated zest of 1 orange

1 teaspoon almond extract

1 teaspoon vanilla paste or extract

1 tablespoon Cointreau liqueur

3 eggs

120ml *(½ cup)* milk (you can also use almond milk for a nutty flavour)

90g *(3½oz)* ground hazelnuts

60g *(2oz)* finely chopped almonds

Icing *(confectioner's)* sugar, for dusting

Method

Preheat the oven to 170°C/335°F. Carefully grease the insides of a bundt tin with butter, making sure you coat every corner. Dust with flour, then tilt and rotate the tin to coat the insides evenly, tipping out the excess.

Sift the measured flour into a bowl, add the baking powder and set aside.

Put the sugar, cinnamon, cloves, nutmeg, orange zest, almond extract and vanilla in the bowl of a stand mixer (or into a mixing bowl, and use electric hand-held beaters) and beat on a low speed to allow the spices to blend and coat the sugar. The smell will be divine at this point!

Add the butter and beat on a medium speed until fluffy. Add the Cointreau and continue beating. Now beat in the eggs, one at a time. When all the ingredients are incorporated, fold in the flour and baking powder mixture, and the milk, in three small additions and alternating them. Finally, fold in the ground hazelnuts and chopped almonds.

Transfer the mixture to the prepared tin and bake for 40–45 minutes until a skewer inserted in the cake comes out clean. Leave to cool in the tin for 10 minutes before inverting on to a plate. When cool, dust with icing sugar to serve, or top with sugar-coated cranberries, holly, or any other decoration you fancy.

LOAF AL LIMONE PINOLI E MANDORLE

LEMON AND PINE NUT DRIZZLE LOAF

I have yet to meet a person who is not addicted to a good slice of moist lemon drizzle cake, and here is the classic version with a twist added in the form of pine nuts. This simple but delicious loaf, with its tangy, fresh flavours, will not fail to impress.

Serves 8–10

Ingredients

230g (*1 cup*) butter, at room temperature, plus extra for greasing

115g (*scant 1 cup*) plain (*all-purpose*) flour

1 teaspoon baking powder

¼ teaspoon salt

250g (*1¼ cups*) caster (*granulated*) sugar

Finely grated zest and juice of 2 lemons

225g (*8oz*) marzipan, kneaded until smooth and cut into small pieces

5 eggs

1 teaspoon vanilla paste or extract

75g (*3oz*) chopped almonds

75g (*3oz*) pine nuts, plus extra to decorate

Icing (*confectioner's*) sugar, for dusting

For the lemon drizzle

80ml (*⅓ cup*) lemon juice

250g (*1¼ cups*) granulated sugar

Method

Preheat the oven to 180°C/350°F. Butter the base and sides of a 1lb loaf tin and line with baking parchment.

Sift the flour, baking powder and salt into a bowl and, using a balloon whisk, stir to combine, then set aside.

Put the sugar, lemon zest and juice in the bowl of a stand mixer, or a mixing bowl and use electric hand-held beaters, and beat on a low speed to coat the sugar nicely. Add the butter and beat until combined, then add the marzipan and beat until the mixture is light and fluffy.

Now add the eggs, one at a time, then the vanilla. Beat to combine. Add the flour mixture and beat just to combine; do not over-beat. Finally, fold in the chopped almonds. Transfer the mixture to the prepared tin, sprinkle the pine nuts over the surface and bake for 45 minutes until a skewer inserted in the middle comes out clean.

Invert the cooked loaf on to a wire rack. In a glass or jug, mix the lemon juice and sugar for the drizzle and pour over the warm loaf, allowing the drizzle to soak into the loaf completely. Dust with icing sugar and top with a few more pine nuts.

FETTE ALL'ANANAS
PINEAPPLE SQUARES

Pineapple is thought to have amazing effects on our body. If consumed regularly it can burn fat and, even better, it contributes to a positive uplifting mood. So, let's bake a pineapple slice and smile!

Makes 6 large slices

Ingredients

170g (¾ cup) butter,
at room temperature,
plus extra for greasing

170g (¾ cup) caster
(granulated) sugar

2 eggs

250g (2 cups) plain
(all-purpose) flour

200ml (¾ cup plus
1 tablespoon) buttermilk

1 teaspoon vanilla paste
or extract

1 teaspoon almond extract

450g (1lb) canned pineapple
in natural juice

For the almond crumble

80g (⅔ cup) plain (all-purpose)
flour

60g (½ cup) light brown sugar

55g (¼ cup) butter, chilled
and diced

30g (1½oz) flaked (slivered)
almonds

Method

Preheat the oven to 180°C/350°F. Butter a 20 x 30-cm/8 x 12-inch brownie tin and line with baking parchment.

Prepare the crumble. In a food processor, pulse the flour, sugar and butter until crumbly. Stir in the slivered almonds by hand and set aside.

In the bowl of a stand mixer, or in a mixing bowl and using hand-held electric beaters, beat the butter and sugar together until pale. Beat in the eggs one at a time. Fold in the flour, buttermilk, vanilla and almond extract to combine.

Spread the mixture into the prepared tin. Open the pineapple can, drain off the juice and roughly chop the pineapple. Spread the pineapple over the top of the mixture in the brownie tin and sprinkle with the almond crumble. Bake in the oven for about 40 minutes until the almond crumble is golden, then leave to cool in the tin on a wire rack before cutting into squares or slices.

TORTA ALLA LAVANDA E MIELE

LAVENDER AND HONEY CAKE

I was born in a big city, but since I moved to the small Italian town of Sarzana, near the World Heritage Site of the Cinque Terre, I've realized how amazing nature is. In cities, everything is processed and ready packed, fruits and vegetables are available all year round and somehow it's easy to forget we are part of a natural cycle. I am now so lucky to have the chance to witness the miracle of the changing seasons. Organic products are everywhere and lavender grows wild – the smell is absolutely incredible.

So it comes naturally to me to bake using the beautiful bounty this land has to offer. The honey I use here is from my monthly supply from my dear friend and beekeeper Lorenzo. But even without a Lorenzo in your life, you can find amazing honeys in wholefood shops. This cake will make a stunning centrepiece for a birthday party in the garden.

Serves 10–12

Ingredients

280g *(2 cups)* plain *(all-purpose)* flour

200g *(1 cup)* caster *(granulated)* sugar

1½ teaspoons baking powder

4 eggs, separated

100ml *(⅓ cup plus 1½ tablespoons)* sunflower oil

100ml *(⅓ cup plus 1½ tablespoons)* water

1 teaspoon lavender oil or natural lavender extract

½ teaspoon pure almond extract

1 tablespoon clear honey

A pinch of salt

¼ teaspoon cream of tartar

For the frosting

250ml *(1 cup plus 1 tablespoon)* double *(heavy)* cream

250g *(9oz)* mascarpone cheese

1 tablespoon clear honey

90g *(¾ cup)* icing *(confectioner's)* sugar

Edible lavender flowers, to decorate

Method

Preheat the oven to 180°C/350°F. Line two 20-cm/8-inch cake tins with baking parchment.

Sift the flour into a bowl and add half the sugar and the baking powder. Put the egg yolks, oil, water, lavender and almond extracts, honey and salt in a separate bowl and beat until just barely combined.

Using a wooden spoon or spatula, add the dry ingredients in small additions, until fully incorporated. At this point, the mixture will be stiff, but it will loosen up once you start adding the egg whites.

Put the eggs whites and cream of tartar into the bowl of a stand mixer fitted with a whisk attachment, or into a mixing bowl and use an electric hand-held whisk, and whisk to stiff peaks. Add a little of the whisked whites to the cake mixture, to loosen, then gently fold in the remaining whisked whites. Divide the mixture evenly between the tins and bake for 20–25 minutes until a skewer inserted in the cakes comes out clean. Leave to cool in the tins for 10 minutes before inverting on to a wire rack.

For the frosting, whisk the cream in a bowl, using a hand-held electric whisk, until medium-stiff. Add the mascarpone and honey and whisk for 1 minute. Finally add the icing sugar and whisk until incorporated. Spread half of the frosting onto one of the cakes. Place the other cake on top and, using a spatula, spread the remaining frosting over the top and sides. Decorate with lavender flowers.

TART ALLA CREMA ED ACQUA DI ROSE

CREAM AND ROSE WATER TART

My bakery and tea room is the result of all the experiences I have had during my life. It's all in there – the people I have met during my travels, the beautiful places I have seen, all the things I have learned, and my other passion, apart from my job, interior design.

It was during a journey in Sri Lanka that I had the chance to try rose water for the first time, in the form of rose water custard. So creamy and scented, it was love at first taste! This tart reminds me of those glorious places, and the smell of rose water takes me back in time... to a land of great treasures.

Serves 8

Ingredients

For the pastry

300g *(scant 2½ cups)* plain *(all-purpose)* flour, plus extra for dusting

150g *(scant ⅔ cup)* butter, chilled and diced, plus extra, softened, for greasing

120g *(½ cup plus 2 tablespoons)* caster *(granulated)* sugar

1 whole egg plus 2 egg yolks

Finely grated zest of 1 lemon

A pinch of salt

For the rose water cream

3 eggs

70g *(½ cup)* plain *(all-purpose)* flour

200g *(1 cup)* caster *(granulated)* sugar

7 tablespoons butter, melted

½ teaspoon vanilla paste or extract

2 teaspoons rose water

240ml *(1 cup)* double *(heavy)* cream

Edible rose petals, to decorate (for a luxurious look), or fresh raspberries (for a more rustic and summery feel)

Method

Put the flour for the pastry in a mound on the work surface and make a well in the centre. Add the diced butter to the well and, working quickly with cool hands, rub it into the flour with your fingertips until the mixture resembles fine breadcrumbs. Make a well again in the centre and place the sugar, whole egg and yolks, lemon zest and salt in the well. Knead the mixture to form a dough, then wrap in cling film (plastic wrap) and refrigerate for at least a couple of hours or, better still, overnight. (You can make the pastry in a food processor if you like, but by hand will produce better results.)

Butter and flour a loose-based, fluted, rectangular tart tin 35 x 11cm/13¾ x 4¼ inches, or a 23-cm/9-inch round, loose-based, fluted tin and preheat the oven to 180°C/350°F.

Roll the dough out on a floured surface to about 3mm/⅛ inch thick and use to line the tart tin, pressing it gently into the grooves. Trim the excess pastry from the edges using a knife, prick the base with a fork in several places and refrigerate while you make the cream.

Whisk the eggs in a bowl and gradually whisk in the flour until combined, then add the sugar, melted butter, vanilla, rose water and cream and stir to combine. Remove the tart case from the fridge, pour in the cream and bake for about 35 minutes or until the pastry is golden.

Leave to cool in the tin before unmoulding on to a plate and decorating as you wish.

TORTA AL CACAO TOSTATO

ROASTED COCOA CAKE

I am a big fan of roasted food: roasted bread, roasted nuts, roasted vegetables and even roasted fruits (yes, you can roast fruits: try drizzling honey over halved figs and roasting them in a hot oven for 10 minutes and you'll see). Cocoa is no exception. When roasted, it releases precious oils and deepens in colour, producing a more complex and stronger flavour than you will find in regular chocolate cake.

It is an easy cake to make, and perfect for people who are egg intolerant. It also makes a good base for many variations: let your inner baker decide!

Serves 10

Ingredients

3 tablespoons vegetable oil, plus extra for greasing

80g (¾ cup) good-quality cocoa powder

200g (1½ cups plus 2 tablespoons) plain (all-purpose) flour, sifted

3 teaspoons baking powder

½ teaspoon bicarbonate of soda (baking soda)

200g (1 cup) caster (granulated) sugar

450ml (scant 2 cups) milk (use soy to make a vegan cake)

1 teaspoon vanilla paste or extract

1 teaspoon Frangelico liqueur (optional, but really enhances the nutty flavour of the roasted cocoa)

Icing (confectioner's) sugar, for dusting (optional)

Method

Preheat the oven to 160°C/320°F. Lightly oil a 20-cm/8-inch cake tin and line with baking parchment.

Line a lipped baking tray with a sheet of baking parchment. Spread the cocoa powder out in an even layer about 5mm/¼ inch thick and bake for 20 minutes, stirring every 5 minutes to avoid burning and to ensure even roasting. When it has turned properly dark, remove from the oven and leave to cool.

Put the cooled roasted cocoa in a large bowl along with the flour, baking powder, bicarbonate of soda and sugar.

In a jug or a separate bowl, whisk the milk, oil, vanilla and Frangelico, if using, together. Lightly mix the dry ingredients into the wet, without over-mixing. Pour into the prepared tin and bake for about 40 minutes until a skewer inserted in the middle comes out clean. Remove to a wire rack and leave to cool in the tin. Invert on to a plate and dust with icing sugar, or serve as it is with a dollop of whipped cream if you prefer.

BISCOTTI AL CIOCCOLATO SENZA GLUTINE CROCCANTI

CRUNCHY GLUTEN-FREE CHOCOLATE COOKIES

These cookies are gluten-free, but no less tasty for it. Nothing more to say... Ah, yes, just one piece of advice: dunk them into a glass of cold milk!

Makes about 20

Ingredients

500g *(3 cups plus 1 tablespoon)* gluten-free icing *(confectioner's)* sugar

90g *(¾ cup plus 1 tablespoon)* gluten-free cocoa powder

1½ tablespoons cornflour *(cornstarch)* or potato flour

¼ teaspoon salt

1 whole egg plus 2 egg whites

1 teaspoon vanilla paste or extract

160g *(1 cup)* gluten-free dark chocolate chips

Method

Preheat the oven to 160°C/320°F. Line two baking sheets with baking parchment.

Put the icing sugar, cocoa, cornflour and salt into the bowl of a stand mixer and stir using a spoon to combine. Attach the paddle tool to the mixer. Add the whole egg and egg whites with the vanilla paste and beat on a low speed. Once properly combined, fold in the chocolate chips.

Using an ice cream scoop, drop dollops of dough onto the baking sheets, spacing them well apart to allow room for spreading. Bake for about 15 minutes. Leave to cool on the sheets before eating.

TART AI LAMPONI E FROLLA AI SEMI DI PAPAVERO

RASPBERRY TART WITH POPPY SEED PASTRY

Everything about this tart is just beautiful! The colour of the raspberries, the specks of poppy seed, the tanginess of the filling! Every time I make it for my customers it sells out in a matter of minutes, and when I have friends over for dinner, it makes people smile with joy!

You can replace the raspberries with blueberries or even blackberries. For a rustic, chic look and a fabulous aroma, garnish with some edible lavender sprigs.

Serves 8

Ingredients

For the pastry

300g *(scant 2½ cups)* plain *(all-purpose)* flour, plus extra for dusting

150g *(scant ⅔ cup)* butter, chilled and diced, plus extra, softened, for greasing

120g *(½ cup plus 2 tablespoons)* caster *(granulated)* sugar

1 whole egg plus 2 egg yolks

Finely grated zest of 1 lemon

80g *(3oz)* poppy seeds

A pinch of salt

2 tablespoons seedless raspberry jam, warmed and strained

For the filling

250g *(9oz)* mascarpone cheese

250ml *(1 cup)* double *(heavy)* cream

6 tablespoons caster *(granulated)* sugar

1 teaspoon vanilla extract

About 450g *(1lb)* raspberries

Method

For the pastry, pile the flour onto the work surface in a mound and make a well in the middle. Add the diced butter and rub into the flour with your fingertips until the mixture resembles fine breadcrumbs. Make a well again and add the sugar, whole egg and yolks, lemon zest, poppy seeds and salt to the well.

Knead until the mixture forms a dough, then wrap in cling film (plastic wrap) and refrigerate for at least a couple of hours or, better still, overnight.

Butter a 23-cm/9-inch fluted, loose-based tart tin and dust with flour. Roll out the chilled dough on a lightly floured surface to about 3mm/⅛ inch thick and use to line the tart tin, pressing it gently into the grooves. Prick the base with a fork in a few places and trim the excess pastry around the edges. Chill in the fridge for about 30 minutes.

Meanwhile, preheat the oven to 180°C/350°F. Place a disc of baking parchment in the pastry case and fill with baking beans. Blind bake for 20–25 minutes, until golden, dry and cooked. Remove from the oven, take out the beans and parchment disc and brush the base with the raspberry jam (to prevent a soggy base). Set aside to cool completely.

For the filling, put the mascarpone, cream, sugar and vanilla into a bowl and beat together well using a wooden spoon, making sure the mascarpone is fully broken down and incorporated. Spread the mixture into the cooled tart case, then cover with cling film (plastic wrap) and refrigerate for about 1½ hours.

When ready to serve, remove the tart from the tin and place on a plate or cake stand. Arrange the raspberries on top and serve.

BISCOTTI D'INVERNO
WINTER COOKIES

I love winter. I love rain and snow, and I love comfort food. These cookies have the fragrance of a warm, cosy night at home, sipping a cup of tea or coffee and watching a movie. Give me my cats, too, and I'm in heaven!

Makes about 20

Ingredients

150g (*scant ⅔ cup*) butter, at room temperature

100g (*½ cup*) caster (*granulated*) sugar

A pinch of salt

¼ teaspoon ground nutmeg

Finely grated zest of 1 orange

2 egg yolks

250g (*2 cups*) plain (*all-purpose*) flour, plus extra for dusting

80g (*¼ cup plus 1 tablespoon*) demerara sugar

Method

In the bowl of a stand mixer, or in a mixing bowl and using hand-held electric beaters, beat the butter and caster sugar together until fluffy. Add the salt, nutmeg, orange zest and one of the egg yolks. Add the flour and beat until a dough is formed. Transfer the dough to a lightly floured surface and knead to form a log. Wrap in cling film (plastic wrap) and refrigerate for at least 1 hour (or overnight).

Preheat the oven to 200°C/400°F and line a baking sheet with baking parchment. In a large shallow dish, briefly whisk the remaining egg yolk. Remove the dough from the fridge and roll it through the egg yolk to coat. (Alternatively, brush the egg yolk all over the log using a pastry brush.) Roll the log through the demerara sugar until fully coated.

Slice the log into about 6-mm/¼-inch rounds and transfer to the prepared baking sheet. Bake for 10–15 minutes until lightly golden. Leave to cool on the baking sheet.

LOAF ALLA ROSA E FRANGIPANE

ROSE AND FRANGIPANE LOAF

I remember finding things not very easy at all during my early attempts as a baker. Life is strange: I ended up doing one of the last things I ever thought I would do. I was scared of baking, scared to fail. Everybody used to say: "Baking is a science and you are very bad at science and maths!" They were right in a way, but after years of studying the subject (because of course you do have to study first), I developed my own way of baking. I would refer to myself as a "punk baker". That said, I am now able to create recipes mixing and matching ingredients in a way I never thought I would be able to do, and this recipe is an example of that. I reckon loaf cakes are underestimated; they are super-fun to make and the possibilities are endless. Try them: enjoy creating interesting combinations using a base recipe, such as a pound cake recipe. Become a "punk baker" too! Have a loaf tea party, where you create a dessert table piled high with different loaf cakes and you'll see how much fun they are!

Serves 8–10

Ingredients

200g *(scant 1 cup)* butter, at room temperature, plus extra for greasing

250g *(2 cups)* plain *(all-purpose)* flour, plus extra for dusting

1½ teaspoons baking powder

A pinch of salt

150g *(¾ cup)* brown sugar

1 teaspoon vanilla paste or extract

1 teaspoon rose water

4 eggs

125g *(4½oz)* marzipan, cut into small pieces

Method

Preheat the oven to 160°C/320°F. Butter a 1lb loaf tin and dust with flour.

Sift the flour, baking powder and salt together and set aside.

In the bowl of a stand mixer, or in a mixing bowl and using electric hand-held beaters, beat the butter and sugar together until fluffy. Beat in the vanilla and rose water, then beat in the eggs, one at a time. Next, beat in the marzipan. When combined, gradually add the flour mixture with the beaters on a low speed, but do not over-mix.

Pour the mixture into the prepared tin and bake for 40–45 minutes until a skewer inserted in the middle comes out clean. Remove from the oven and leave to cool in the tin for about 20 minutes before inverting on to a wire rack to cool completely.

LOAF AL CIOCCOLATO, BASILICO E PEPE DI SICHUAN

CHOCOLATE, BASIL AND SICHUAN PEPPER LOAF CAKE

This is an explosion of exotic flavours. Basil is my favourite herb in the entire world – I eat the leaves all summer straight from the big plant I grow on my terrace, so it was just natural for me to develop a cake recipe using basil. Sichuan pepper (which isn't actually a pepper, but is so called because its berries resemble black peppercorns) is widely used in China and can be found in almost every supermarket these days. I recommend you grind it yourself, with a pestle and mortar or in a spice grinder, for a full flavour.

Serves 8–10

Ingredients

200g *(scant 1 cup)* butter, at room temperature, plus extra for greasing

50g *(½ cup)* good-quality cocoa powder, plus extra for dusting

250g *(2 cups)* plain *(all-purpose)* flour

1 teaspoon baking powder

½ teaspoon bicarbonate of soda *(baking soda)*

200g *(1 cup)* caster *(granulated)* sugar

4 eggs

90ml *(⅓ cup plus 2 teaspoons)* milk

A bunch of fresh basil leaves, finely chopped

½ teaspoon ground Sichuan pepper

Method

Preheat the oven to 160°C/320°F. Butter a 1lb loaf tin and dust with cocoa powder.

Sift the flour, baking powder and bicarbonate of soda into a bowl and set aside.

In the bowl of a stand mixer, or in a mixing bowl and using hand-held electric beaters, beat the butter and sugar together until light and fluffy. Add the cocoa powder and beat on a low speed until combined. Beat in the eggs one at a time. Once incorporated, stir in the flour mixture and milk alternately in three additions, starting and ending with the flour.

Finally, stir in the basil and Sichuan pepper. Pour the mixture into the prepared tin and bake for 40–45 minutes until a skewer inserted into the middle comes out clean. Remove from the oven and leave to cool in the tin for 10 minutes before inverting on to a wire rack. Dust with cocoa powder and serve.

LOAF AL LIMONE E TIMO

LEMON AND THYME LOAF

This is a super-fresh and super-scented breakfast treat. I have a slice of cake every day, either for breakfast or tea, and I do not intend to stop. I truly believe cakes and desserts are an important part of our lives. Of course, as for everything, they should be consumed in moderation but what would life be like without a piece of cake? So, forget about chemicals, preservatives and other harmful ingredients and go for the real, fresh deal, homemade or bought from a local, trusted bakery. In Italy we get to know the people we buy from. They are happy because they create a bond with the customer and I am happy because I know I will be treated well. Someone once said: think global, eat local. This has become my mantra.

Serves about 10

Ingredients

210g *(1½ cups)* plain *(all-purpose)* flour

A pinch of salt

2¼ teaspoons baking powder

3 tablespoons finely chopped fresh thyme leaves, plus extra (optional) to serve

2 eggs, at room temperature

Grated zest of 2 large lemons

240ml *(1 cup)* full-fat Greek yogurt

250g *(1¼ cups)* caster *(granulated)* sugar

1 teaspoon vanilla paste or extract

150ml *(½ cup plus 2 tablespoons)* vegetable oil

For the syrup

115g *(½ cup plus 1 tablespoon)* caster *(granulated)* sugar

115ml *(½ cup)* lemon juice

Method

Preheat the oven to 170°C/335°F. Line the base and sides of a 1lb loaf tin with baking parchment.

In a bowl, sift together the flour, salt and baking powder and stir in the chopped thyme. In a separate bowl, whisk together the eggs, lemon zest, yogurt, sugar, vanilla and oil until well blended. Gently add the dry ingredients to the wet ingredients and combine. Pour the mixture into the lined tin and bake for 40–45 minutes until golden on top and a skewer inserted into the centre comes out clean.

While the cake is baking, prepare the syrup. Put the sugar and lemon juice in a saucepan over a medium heat until the sugar is fully dissolved.

Leave the cake in its tin to cool for 15 minutes, then invert onto a wire rack. Using a wooden toothpick or skewer, prick the surface of the cake and carefully drizzle the syrup over to allow the juice to penetrate inside the cake. Leave to cool completely before sprinkling with thyme, if you like, and cutting into slices to serve.

TORTA PARADISO

PARADISE CAKE

This gluten-free and sugar-free chocolate cake (also free of raising agents) is a hit down at my bakery and tea room. The reason? It is simply amazing! The consistency is a cross between a cake and a mousse – my customers love it and I hope you will too.

The cake itself is very basic, but in order to achieve perfect results, follow the recipe very carefully, as its success lies in the method.

Serves 8–10

Ingredients

230g (1 cup) butter, diced, plus extra, softened, for greasing

450g (1lb) good-quality dark, sugar-free chocolate, chopped into small pieces

1 teaspoon vanilla paste or extract

8 eggs, fridge-cold

Good-quality cocoa powder, for dusting

Method

Preheat the oven to 170°C/335°F. Butter the base and sides of a 20-cm/8-inch deep springform cake tin and line the base with baking parchment. Brush some butter on the baking parchment and wrap foil tightly all around the outside of the tin to make it watertight. Set aside.

Put the chocolate and butter in a large heatproof bowl set over a pan of barely simmering water, making sure the bowl isn't touching the water. Leave until completely melted, stirring occasionally, then remove the bowl from the pan, stir in the vanilla and set aside to cool slightly.

Meanwhile, put the eggs in the bowl of a stand mixer fitted with a whisk attachment (or use a mixing bowl and electric hand-held whisk) and whisk for about 10 minutes, until quadrupled in volume. Gently fold a small amount of whisked egg into the melted chocolate mixture. Once incorporated, add the rest of the whisked egg in three separate additions, folding in each very gently until fully incorporated.

Pour the mixture into the cake tin, without pressing or spreading it. Place the tin inside a larger one and fill the larger one with hot water to come about halfway up the wrapped tin. This is a water bath and it helps to bake the cake gently and evenly. Transfer to the oven and bake for about 20–25 minutes, until cooked but the middle still has a wobble. Lift the cake tin from the water and place on a wire rack. Very gently remove the foil and leave the cake to cool until the tin is cool to the touch, then transfer to the fridge to chill.

Once chilled (and not before), run the tip of a sharp knife around the inside of the tin and release the cake from the tin. Put back in the fridge until ready to serve, then sift over a dusting of cocoa powder, cut into slices and serve with cream.

PRALINE AL COCCO
COCONUT PRALINES

Are you in search of a super-easy, super-quick recipe for those last-minute dinner parties or kids' play dates? Well, look no further: here it is, and you don't even need to use your oven. Coconut can be a tricky ingredient, as some people love it and others hate it. I am right in the middle, as I don't like it in every dessert. Chocolate and coconut? Yes, yes! Coconut ice cream? No, no! In this recipe the coconut flavour is subtle and the cocoa powder and amaretti biscuits add an unexpected twist. Plus there is also the queen of cheeses for baking: ricotta… "she" makes everything taste divine, but what can I say? I'm Italian!

Makes about 25

Ingredients

250g *(9oz)* ricotta cheese

2 tablespoons crushed amaretti cookies

100g *(3½oz)* coconut flour

50g *(½ cup)* good-quality cocoa powder

100g *(½ cup)* caster *(granulated)* sugar

100g *(⅓ cup plus 1½ tablespoons)* butter, at room temperature

100g *(3½oz)* finely shredded desiccated coconut

Method

Put the ricotta, amaretti, coconut flour, cocoa powder, sugar and butter in a large bowl and knead, using your hands, until fully combined.

Cover the bowl with cling film (plastic wrap) and refrigerate for at least 1 hour or until set enough to shape.

Using your hands, roll the mixture into balls the size of truffles, then roll each ball in the desiccated coconut to coat evenly all over. Place on a tray and store in the fridge until ready to serve.

TORTA A STRATI COCCO E ANANAS

COCONUT PINEAPPLE LAYER CAKE

This is a cake I make for the tea room during the summer. It is fresh, full of aroma and has a very soft texture. You can make it for a birthday party, or simply to impress friends. The recipe is so versatile that you can change it as you please. And what to say about coconut? There's nothing more summery than coconut, so let's indulge, with no further ado…

Serves 8–12

Ingredients

For the filling

400g (*2 cups*) caster (*granulated*) sugar

30g (*¼ cup*) cornflour (*cornstarch*)

240ml (*1 cup*) canned crushed pineapple in juice

240ml (*1 cup*) water

For the cakes

A little softened butter, for greasing

285g (*2 cups plus 2 tablespoons*) plain (*all-purpose*) flour

1½ teaspoons baking powder

200g (*1 cup*) caster (*granulated*) sugar

4 eggs, separated

¼ teaspoon cream of tartar

A pinch of salt

100ml (*scant ½ cup*) vegetable oil

100ml (*scant ½ cup*) water

Grated zest of 1 lemon

1 teaspoon vanilla paste or extract

¼ teaspoon pure organic coconut extract

300ml (*1¼ cups*) crushed pineapple in juice

Desiccated coconut, to finish

For the frosting

200g (*scant 1 cup*) butter, at room temperature

500g (*1lb 2oz*) cream cheese, at room temperature

150g (*1¼ cups*) icing (*confectioner's*) sugar

Method

Make the filling. Stir together the sugar and cornflour in a saucepan, add the pineapple and water and cook over a low heat, stirring occasionally, for about 15 minutes or until thick. Set aside to cool. For the cakes, preheat the oven to 180°C/350°F. Butter two 20-cm/8-inch cake tins and line the bases with baking parchment.

Sift the flour into a medium bowl, add the baking powder and half the sugar and whisk to combine. Put the egg yolks in the bowl of a stand mixer fitted with a paddle attachment. Add the salt, oil, water, lemon zest, vanilla, coconut extract and pineapple with its juice to the egg yolks, and beat until mixed, then add the flour and sugar mixture and beat for 1 more minute or until well incorporated (but do not over-mix).

Add the cream of tartar to the egg whites and, using an electric hand-held whisk, whisk until frothy. Add the remaining sugar and whisk to stiff peaks. Very gently fold the whisked egg whites into the egg yolk mixture. Divide the mixture between the prepared tins and bake for 20–25 minutes until a skewer inserted in the middle comes out clean. Invert the cakes on to a wire rack and leave to cool.

For the frosting, put the butter into the bowl of a stand mixer, or into a mixing bowl and using electric hand-held beaters, and beat until creamy. Add the cream cheese and beat until combined. Finally, beat in the icing sugar.

To assemble, place one cooled cake on a cake board or plate. Spread half the pineapple filling over and top with the second cake. Spread the remaining filling over the top. Spread the frosting onto the sides of the cake. Sprinkle all over with coconut flour or shavings.

TORTA AL LIMONE E MASCARPONE

LEMON AND MASCARPONE CAKE

I know, I know… another lemon cake! But this is no ordinary lemon cake: the texture is so light and the taste so fresh that you really need to try it! Every time I bake this at the bakery, it sells fast. Use organic lemons here, as they will make all the difference.

Serves 12–14

Ingredients

For the mascarpone frosting

250ml (*1 cup plus 2 teaspoons*) double (*heavy*) cream

90g (*½ cup plus 1 tablespoon*) icing (*confectioner's*) sugar

250g (*9oz*) mascarpone cheese

3 teaspoons finely grated lemon zest

For the cake

A little softened butter, for greasing

285g (*2 cups plus 2 tablespoons*) plain (*all-purpose*) flour

1½ teaspoons baking powder

200g (*1 cup*) caster (*granulated*) sugar

4 eggs, separated

¼ teaspoon cream of tartar

A pinch of salt

100ml (*scant ½ cup*) vegetable oil

100ml (*scant ½ cup*) water, at room temperature

Grated zest of 4 lemons

1 teaspoon pure lemon extract

1 teaspoon vanilla paste or extract

Fresh fruit or lemon curd, to decorate (optional)

Method

Prepare the mascarpone frosting. In the bowl of a stand mixer, whisk the cream and icing sugar until medium stiff. Change to the paddle attachment on the stand mixer and, in the same bowl, beat the mascarpone until creamy. Add the lemon zest and beat to incorporate. Put the bowl in the fridge until ready to use.

Preheat the oven to 180°C/350°F. Butter two 20-cm/8-inch cake tins and line the bases and sides with baking parchment.

Sift the flour into a medium bowl, add the baking powder and half the sugar and whisk to combine. Set aside. Put the egg whites and cream of tartar in a large bowl and set aside.

Put the yolks in the bowl of a stand mixer fitted with a paddle attachment. Add the salt, oil, water, lemon zest and extract, and vanilla and beat until mixed, then add the flour mixture and beat for 1 minute or until well mixed (do not over-mix).

Using an electric hand-held whisk, whisk the egg whites until frothy, then add the remaining sugar and whisk until stiff peaks form. Fold the whisked egg whites very gently into the cake batter then divide the mixture between the prepared tins and bake in the oven for 20–25 minutes until a skewer inserted into the middle comes out clean. Remove from the oven and leave to cool on a wire rack.

To assemble, spread a generous layer of the mascarpone frosting over one of the cakes. Place the second cake on top and spread the frosting over the top and sides. (Alternatively, you can cut each cake in half horizontally to give 4 layers of cake, spreading frosting between each layer.) Decorate with fresh fruit or pipe a crown of frosting around the edges and fill with lemon curd. Put the cake in the fridge until ready to serve.

BISCOTTI RIPIENI ALLA CREMA DI NOCCIOLE

HAZELNUT-FILLED COOKIES

These hazelnut-filled cookies are all it takes to crown you teatime goddess! They are very, very easy to make, with the cream giving them a soft centre. If you want to play with different combinations, swap the hazelnut spread for lemon curd or jam.

Makes 15–20, depending on size

Ingredients

300g (*scant 2½ cups*) plain (*all-purpose*) flour, plus extra for dusting

150g (*1 cup plus 2 tablespoons*) rice flour

A pinch of salt

120g (*½ cup plus 2 tablespoons*) caster (*granulated*) sugar

1 whole egg plus 1 egg yolk

1 teaspoon vanilla paste or extract

1 teaspoon baking powder (*baking soda*)

250g (*1 cup plus 2 tablespoons*) butter, at room temperature

1 jar of organic hazelnut spread

Icing (*confectioner's*) sugar, for dusting

Method

Place both flours with the salt, sugar, whole egg plus yolk, vanilla and baking powder in the bowl of a stand mixer fitted with a paddle attachment. On a low speed, mix the ingredients together until well combined, then add the softened butter and beat on a high speed until the mixture comes together in a dough.

Transfer to a lightly floured surface, knead just enough to bring the dough together, then wrap in cling film (plastic wrap) and chill in the fridge for at least 1 hour.

Meanwhile, preheat oven to 180°C/350°F and line a large baking sheet with baking parchment.

Roll out the chilled dough to about a 5-mm/ ¼-inch thickness. Using a round cookie cutter, stamp out 40 rounds. Using a teaspoon, scoop a little hazelnut spread on the centre of 20 of the rounds, then place the remaining 20 rounds on top, pressing down gently. Transfer the assembled cookies to the lined baking sheet and bake for 8–10 minutes, until just lightly golden.

Remove from the oven and leave to cool on the baking sheet before removing and dusting with icing sugar.

CROSTATA DI MARMELLATA SENZA GLUTINE

GLUTEN-FREE JAM TART

I know a person (or perhaps many) who will thank me for this recipe. It is very simple with a rustic feel, and is also gluten-free. It can be used as base for endless variations, playing with different jam flavours or using a chocolate ganache filling. For this version I use fruit jam, not only because it is *soooo* good, but also because "you can never eat enough of it" (you know I'm talking about you, V, so this is dedicated to you, my darling friend and assistant). If possible, make your own jam using organic fruit, or buy the best available. It makes a huge difference.

Serves 6

Ingredients

300g *(2 cups)* rice flour, plus extra for dusting

150g *(1¼ cups plus 1 tablespoon)* fine cornflour *(cornstarch)*

180g *(¾ cup plus 2 tablespoons)* caster *(granulated)* sugar

2 eggs

150g *(⅔ cup)* butter, softened and cut into small pieces, plus extra for greasing

Grated zest of 1 lemon

A pinch of salt

1 jar of your favourite organic jam

Gluten-free icing *(confectioner's)* sugar, for dusting (optional)

Method

Combine both flours and place in a mound on the work surface. Make a well in the middle and add the sugar, eggs, butter, lemon zest and salt to the well. Using a dough spatula or simply your hands, work the ingredients together until they form a dough, making sure your hands are not too hot. If they are, stop kneading, place your hands under cold water, dry them and knead again, adding a little cold water if necessary. Divide the dough in half, wrap each half in cling film (plastic wrap) and refrigerate for at least 30 minutes.

Preheat the oven to 160°C/320°F. Butter a 18-cm/ 7-inch tart tin or shallow baking tin, ideally with a removable base. Dust with a little rice flour and tap out the excess.

Roll out one half of the dough on a surface lightly floured with rice flour, to about 2.5cm/1 inch thick. Transfer to the tart tin, and press gently into place. Prick the base with a fork and spread the entire jar of jam into the pastry case. Refrigerate while you roll out the other half of dough to the same thickness. Using a small heart-shaped (or other) cookie cutter, stamp out about 30–40 cookies. Remove the filled case from the fridge and arrange the pastry cookies around the edge of the tart, overlapping them in 3 concentric rings towards the middle, then placing one in the centre of the exposed jam in the middle.

Bake in the oven for about 30 minutes, or until the pastry is golden and cooked. Serve cut into slices as it is, or dusted with icing sugar.

TART AI FICHI E MASCARPONE

FIG AND MASCARPONE TART

Fig trees grow wild in many areas of Italy, and memories take me back to my uncle and aunty's house in the country. Nearby there were two huge trees, one cherry and the other a fig tree. Every summer my aunty used to make fig jam, and my duty was to go and pick as many figs as I could, but as I never liked figs I would climb the cherry tree and eat tons of cherries instead. Thankfully, tastes change as we grow up, and now I am crazy about figs!

This tart is fresh, summery and full of flavour. Drizzle some clear honey on top of the figs and serve it on a beautiful plate or stand; it is so glorious that it deserves a super-elegant presentation.

Serves 8

Ingredients

For the pastry

300g (*scant 2½ cups*) plain (*all-purpose*) flour, plus extra for dusting

150g (*scant ⅔ cup*) butter, chilled and diced, plus extra for greasing

120g (*½ cup plus 2 tablespoons*) caster (*granulated*) sugar

1 whole egg plus 2 egg yolks

Grated zest of 1 lemon

A pinch of salt

For the mascarpone filling

450g (*1lb*) mascarpone cheese

50g (*¼ cup*) caster (*granulated*) sugar

120ml (*½ cup*) double (*heavy*) cream

1 teaspoon vanilla paste or extract

For the top

About 20 figs (depending on size), quartered

2 tablespoons apricot jam

2 tablespoons clear honey

Method

To make the pastry, put the flour in a mound on the work surface and make a well in the middle. Add the diced butter to the well and, working quickly to keep everything cool, rub it into the flour using your fingertips until the mixture resembles fine breadcrumbs. Make a well again and place the sugar, egg and extra yolks, lemon zest and salt in the well. Knead into a dough, wrap in cling film (plastic wrap) and refrigerate for at least a couple of hours or, better still, overnight. (You can use a food processor to make the pastry, but making it by hand will give better results.)

Preheat the oven to 160°C/320°F. Lightly butter a 23-cm/9-inch loose-based, fluted tart tin and dust with flour. Roll the dough out on a lightly floured surface to about 3mm/⅛ inch thick and use to line the tart tin, pressing it gently into the grooves. Prick the base with a fork in a few places and trim the excess pastry around the edges. Cut out a disc of baking parchment and place it inside the tart, then fill with baking beans and blind bake for about 25 minutes until golden, dry and cooked. Remove from the oven, take out the baking beans and parchment disc and leave to cool completely in the tin, set on a wire rack.

For the filling, whisk the mascarpone, sugar, cream and vanilla in the bowl of a stand mixer fitted with a whisk attachment, or in a mixing bowl using an electric hand-held whisk, taking care not to over-whisk so it is too stiff; it should still be spreadable. Spoon into the cooled pastry case and smooth it out using a spatula.

Arrange the figs on top of the mascarpone filling, fanning out from the centre in a decorative way. Heat the apricot jam and use a pastry brush to brush it over the figs. Drizzle the honey over the entire tart to finish, then cut into slices and serve.

TORTA ALLE PERE CAPOVOLTA

PEAR UPSIDE-DOWN CAKE

Pears are amazing — full of character and flavour, with so many varieties available that baking with them can become a very serious matter of mixing and matching different qualities. For this recipe I use Kaiser or Red Bartlett varieties, as both have a very juicy and scented pulp that makes them ideal for baking. If you can't find them, you can use another variety.

Serves 8

Ingredients

For the cake

150g (*1¼ cups*) plain (*all-purpose*) flour

1½ teaspoons baking powder

¼ teaspoon salt

4 tablespoons polenta (fine cornmeal)

3 medium pears

110g (*just under ½ cup*) butter, at room temperature

150g (*¾ cup*) caster (*granulated*) sugar

1 teaspoon vanilla paste or extract

2 eggs

120ml (*½ cup*) milk

For the caramel

2 tablespoons water

50g (*¼ cup*) caster (*granulated*) sugar

1 tablespoon butter

Method

Preheat the oven to 180°C/350°F. Line a 20-cm/8-inch round cake tin with baking parchment.

Sift the flour, baking powder and salt into a bowl, then stir in the polenta.

For the caramel, put the water into a small pan set over a medium heat and add the sugar. Heat, without stirring, until the sugar has completely dissolved then, swirling the pan once or twice, cook until it turns a dark golden colour, about 9 minutes. Immediately remove the pan from the heat and add the butter. Whisk until blended, then pour the caramel into the prepared tin and swirl to evenly coat the base.

Peel the pears, remove the cores and slice lengthways into thin slices. Arrange the slices in overlapping layers over the caramel.

In the bowl of a stand mixer, or using a mixing bowl and electric hand-held beaters, beat the butter and sugar for the cake together until pale and fluffy. Add the vanilla, then beat in the eggs, one at a time. Fold in the flour mixture and milk in three separate additions, alternating between them. Pour the mixture over the pears in the tin and bake for about 20–25 minutes until a skewer inserted in the middle comes out clean.

Leave to cool in the tin for 45 minutes, then place a large serving plate over the tin and invert the cake. Carefully remove the tin and allow the cake to cool completely before serving.

TORTA VEGANA

VEGAN CAKE

It doesn't matter if you are vegan or not, this cake is a simple and yet wonderful base for all your creations. It also happens to be healthy. Italians are about good food, whether vegan, vegetarian or not. I believe in using a piece of a very good organic butter rather than artificial substitutes, and am aware of keeping my eyes open, as not all vegan ingredients are good for you. But this cake is, as it uses only real ingredients. Bake it with or without chocolate, with or without a layer of jam, but please make sure you bake it!

Serves 8

Ingredients

200g (1½ cups plus 2 tablespoons) unbleached plain (all-purpose) flour, sifted

200g (1 cup) organic vegan white cane sugar

4 tablespoons potato flour

240ml (1 cup) organic soy milk

2 teaspoons organic baking powder

1 teaspoon vanilla paste or extract

Finely grated zest of 1 orange

60ml (¼ cup) organic extra virgin olive oil

100g (3oz) organic vegan dark chocolate chips (optional)

Icing (confectioner's) sugar, for dusting

Method

Preheat the oven to 180°C/350°F. Line a 20-cm/ 8-inch cake tin with baking parchment.

Put the sifted flour, sugar and potato flour in a large bowl. Using a balloon whisk, stir the dry ingredients together, then start adding the soy milk in a steady stream, whisking constantly. Once it is all incorporated, whisk in the baking powder, vanilla and orange zest, and then the oil. Stir in the chocolate chips, if using.

Pour the batter into the prepared tin and bake for about 35 minutes, until lightly golden and a skewer inserted into the centre comes out clean.

Leave to cool completely in the tin before inverting on to a plate. Dust generously with icing sugar and cut into slices to serve.

PALLE D'INVERNO

WINTER SNOWBALL COOKIES

I have already mentioned how much I am into the whole Christmas preparation. Actually, I love the days preceding Christmas more than Christmas Day itself, and in fact on the day, I get a little blue. Probably because of all the anticipation and work we are all engaged in, and once the day comes, Christmas feels over. Oh well, let's focus on the nice part then: baking! The tea room at Christmas explodes with decorations, and the sound of Christmas carols is always present!

These make a perfect gift for friends or colleagues, packaged in a nice bag or box tied with beautiful ribbons.

Makes 24, depending on size

Ingredients

230g *(1 cup)* butter,
at room temperature

110g *(scant 1 cup)* icing
(*confectioner's*) sugar

¼ teaspoon salt

2 teaspoons vanilla paste
or extract

3 tablespoons cornflour
(*cornstarch*)

280g *(2 cups)* plain
(*all-purpose*) flour

1 tablespoon good-quality
cocoa powder

75g *(3oz)* ground almonds

To decorate

About 320g *(2⅔ cups)* icing
(*confectioner's*) sugar

Method

Preheat the oven to 180°C/350°F. Line a baking sheet with baking parchment.

In the bowl of a stand mixer fitted with the paddle attachment, mix the butter on a medium speed until creamy. (Alternatively, use a mixing bowl and a wooden spoon.) Add the icing sugar and salt, mix in the vanilla, sprinkle in the cornflour and, with the mixer on a low speed, slowly add in the flour and cocoa powder and mix just until combined. Finally, stir in ground almonds.

Scoop the dough out, 1 tablespoon at a time, and roll into a ball, placing the balls on the baking sheet. Bake in the oven for 16–18 minutes, until the bottom edges are lightly golden.

Remove from the oven and allow to cool for several minutes then, while they are still warm, tip the icing sugar into a bowl and roll the cookies in it to coat. Transfer to a wire rack to cool, then, once completely cool, roll them in the icing sugar once more, this time to generously coat, pressing the icing sugar on a little.

Index

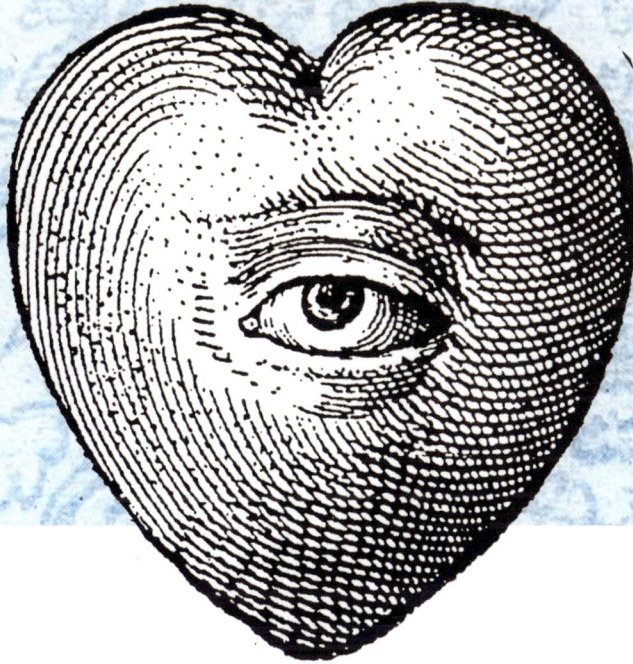

Acknowledgments

With all my heart I wish to thank:

Massimo Zannoni for being my heart and my everything, and for creating the most beautiful graphics in this book – I love you so much. My two beloved black cats! They never left my side during the endless nights in front of my computer writing these recipes. My mother above all, who is my biggest fan. My father and sisters and my adopted family Lucia, Fausto and Marianna. My true friend and amazing assistant Valentina who has believed in me always; for this I love you. Rachele, my precious helper, thank you! Danny Bernardini for your work, patience and friendship. All my friends, especially those who helped me during this project and allowed me to invade their home during the photo shoots: Habiba and Germano, Valentina Giovando, Gabriele Di Sarcina, Francesco and Jess. Serena and Charis my dear supercool BFFs! My kindred spirits, Ale Palermo and Federico C. I want to thank everyone I have met throughout my life – each and every one of you has made me who I am. The city of Sarzana for making feel at home from the first day I arrived in town. All my fans and customers who have supported me over the years! Finally, I wish to thank the amazing team at Quadrille for sharing my vision and for helping me make this dream come true.

Melissa, XXX

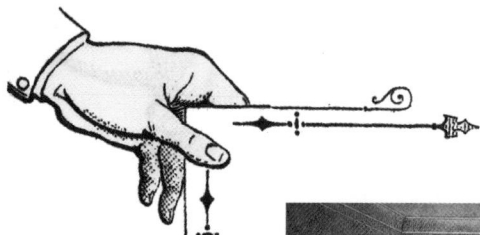

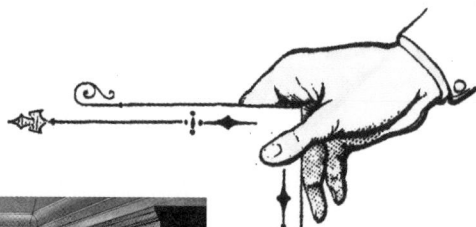

PUBLISHING DIRECTOR: SARAH LAVELLE
CREATIVE DIRECTOR: HELEN LEWIS
SENIOR EDITOR: CÉLINE HUGHES
DESIGNER: MASSIMO ZANNONI
ASSISTANT DESIGNER: EMILY LAPWORTH
PHOTOGRAPHER: DANNY BERNARDINI
PRODUCTION: TOM MOORE, VINCENT SMITH

First published in 2016 by
Quadrille Publishing
Pentagon House
52–54 Southwark Street
London SE1 1UN
www.quadrille.co.uk

Quadrille is an imprint of Hardie Grant
www.hardiegrant.com.au

Cataloguing in Publication Data: a catalogue record
for this book is available from the British Library.

ISBN: 978 184949 761 9

Printed in China